Lazarus!
Come Out!

Lazarus!
Come Out!

Why Faith Needs Imagination

Richard Cote, OMI

NOVALIS

© 2003 Novalis, Saint Paul University, Ottawa, Canada

Cover design: Caroline Gagnon
Cover images: EyeWire (front cover); Richard Cote (back cover)
Layout: Anne Côté
Interior images: p. 15: William Blake (1757–1827). *Elohim Creating Adam.* Tate Gallery, London/Art Resource, NY; p. 35: Herman Falke, *Stations,* photographed by Rob Filion; p. 57: Detail from Pouget, *L'Apothéose d'Auguste,* found in La Ste-Chapelle Royale du Palais, Paris; p. 73: Thomas Cole (1801–1848), *St. John in the Wilderness.* Wadsworth Atheneum, Hartford. Bequest of Daniel Wadsworth; p. 92: Hieronymus Van Aeken Bosch (1450–1516), *The Table of the Seven Deadly Sins,* from the collection of Museo del Prado, Spain; p. 111: Herman Falke, photographed by Rob Filion; p. 134 Bronze statue of Zeus (Poseidon?) in the collection of the National Archaeological Museum of Athens. Reproduced with permission of the Hellenic Ministry of Culture; p. 154: Herman Falke, photographed by Jean-Paul Picard. All images reproduced by permission.

Business Office:
Novalis
49 Front Street East, 2nd Floor
Toronto, Ontario, Canada
M5E 1B3

Phone: 1-800-387-7164 or (416) 363-3303
Fax: 1-800-204-4140 or (416) 363-9409
E-mail: cservice@novalis.ca
www.novalis.ca

National Library of Canada Cataloguing in Publication

Cote, Richard
        Lazarus! Come out! : why faith needs imagination / Richard Cote.

Includes bibliographical references.
ISBN 2-89507-307-4

        1. Imagination–Religious aspects–Christianity. I. Title.

BR115.I6C68 2003   230   C2003-900375-2

Printed in Canada.

We acknowledge the financial support of the Government of Canada through the Book Publishing Industry Development Program (BPIDP) for our publishing activities.

5   4   3   2   1   07   06   05   04   03

Contents

Why Lazarus?

E veryone loves a good story! Ever since I was a little child, the story of Lazarus (John 11:1-45) has been one of my favourites. It contains everything you need to fuel the religious imagination of both young and old: drama, suspense, life, friendship, death, family, bewilderment, boundary-crossing – and a mind-jolting, surprise ending. This gospel story jump-starts the religious imagination as few others do.

For that reason, a strong alliance, a "bond-in-being," is forged between Lazarus, the man from Bethany who was brought back to life by Jesus, and our own long-neglected, 'entombed' religious imagination. As we will discover together in this book, their vibrant story is very similar, their destiny thrillingly intertwined, and their symbolic power much greater than meets the eye.

It is highly appropriate, therefore, that Lazarus should journey with us throughout this study. He will be our trusted guide and will command much of the development in this unfolding story. As someone who symbolizes boundary-crossing at its best, Lazarus will help "awaken" in us our own paschal imagination – that God-given faculty we so often neglect in our life of faith.

Richard Cote

Introduction

The aim of this study is to rehabilitate the religious imagination in our contemporary faith odyssey and to give back to this precious faculty the vibrancy and dynamism it once enjoyed in the spiritual life of the faithful. What is essential to the nature and play of the imagination, I will argue, is essential in our life of faith. To Jesus' question "Who do you say I am?" Christians of every age and every culture have responded with a profession of faith that is at once steeped in both the living tradition of their Church and in their own religious imagination. Until quite recently, theologians have not given much attention to the play of imagination, even in their own theological constructions. This comes as little surprise since the West, for the greater part of its intellectual history, has given pride of place to reason, not imagination. We have generally belittled the imagination by relegating its use to the entertainment world and to a few marginal groups like artists and poets. In our more serious pursuits, we have often regarded it as a deceptive, even dangerous, power. Why dangerous? Because of its presumed will-o'-the-wisp unreliability. The Church, too, has long harboured a mistrust of the imagination by not giving sufficient heed to the imaginal experience of many of its members in the areas of originality, passion, non-rational thought, theopoesis, creativity and playfulness. Neither has imagination figured very prominently in much of her sanctioned vision of reality or magisterial teaching. Typical of such mistrust is Pascal's view of the imagination as a spiritual deceiver: "It is man's ruling faculty, queen of lies and error, and all the greater deceiver since she does not always deceive.... But being most often false she leaves no sure mark of her quality, for she sets the same stamp upon truth and falsehood."[1]

Despite this general deep mistrust of imaginative thinking in the West, and in the Western Church in particular, Christians have never been completely devoid of religious imagination, nor have they ever ceased to make use of it in their life of faith. On the contrary, they seem to have always known – perhaps unconsciously, but with the sure instinct of their faith – that a vital point of contact between divine revelation and human experience resides in the religious imagination. We see this, especially, in the popular piety and spontaneous devotions of the faithful as well as in that special breed of Christians we call the mystics. I say "special breed" because until quite recently they had long been neglected and left out in the cold. Today, the mystics and their writings are reappearing on the shelves of even our secular bookstores. At either end of the spectrum – whether at the grassroots level of the faithful or at the sublime heights of such mystics as Hugh of St. Victor, Bernard of Clairvaux, the admirable Ruysbroeck, John of the Cross, Teresa of Avila – the active imaginations of Christians have managed to survive in the Church, but only marginally.

The choice of Lazarus of Bethany as a symbol or root metaphor for the fate of the religious imagination in recent years is both deliberate and deliberately imaginative. Deliberate, I say, because symbolic imagery is the *first* language of the soul, and rational concepts alone, even in a study such as this, cannot do full justice to the mediating and transcendent role of the imagination in matters of faith and spirituality. When we hear the Word of God, we hear it first and foremost at the level of the imagination. Our choice of Lazarus is also deliberately imaginative because he who visited the land of the dead and was reunited with his beloved village and family at Bethany is eminently qualified to serve as our guide. In a most dramatic way, Lazarus symbolizes "boundary-crossing" which, as we will see in this study, is precisely what the imagination does best: it can transcend any and all boundaries. Herein lies its saving grace. The close resemblance between the fate of Lazarus and that of the religious imagination will thus accompany us throughout this study and will even command much of its development.

Imagination, I hope to show, is not hostile or inimical to faith. To the contrary, it attaches itself to faith as a constitutive dimension of faith itself, an abiding and necessary enticement to believe, hope and love. Imagination can be described as the climate of faith, the condition of its possibility: neither its ground nor its goal of perfection, but a penultimate instrument of grace in a world whose final salvation remains an object of hope. And hope, as we know, is always based on some promise and therefore on the ability to "see" beyond what meets the eye. As St. Paul says, "In hope we were saved. Now hope that is seen is not hope. For who hopes for what is seen?" (Romans 8:24). Hope, like faith, requires considerable imagination. So does love of one's neighbour. How is it possible to love our sometimes unlovable neighbour or to see the face of Christ in the poorest of the poor in our society if we do not draw – at times very heavily – upon our religious imagination? Without religious imagination, is it possible to see the providential hand of God in our lives, especially in our rapidly changing times, or to discern the "in-breaking" signs of God's reign in our world when things look so bleak and unpromising for the future? All three prime Christian virtues – faith, hope and charity – tax and engage the believer's religious imagination much more than we generally assume. It will be the burden of this study to justify this claim. If human imagination is our natural, inborn faculty for transcendence, for going beyond what meets the eye and what we typically call reality – beyond what hitherto seems real and possible – the faithful imagination of Christians (what Sandra M. Schneiders has called the "paschal imagination") opens up unprecedented possibilities for the believer and the Church today.

The resuscitation of the Christian imagination is long overdue, especially if the Church wishes to speak meaningfully to a pilgrim people that is about to embark on yet another lengthy sojourn in the wilderness (Chapter 8). Our central focus in this study will be to contextualize the importance of the religious imagination in our present transitional period, what many are calling one of the great "axial ruptures" in history. Because of the enormous distance that separates us from the founding events of Christianity and the great culture shift we are experiencing in our world today, a bold creative act of the Christian imagination is required to interpret the gospel anew for our rapidly changing times. Without such a creative and imaginative reinterpretation, it is doubtful we can long survive in our new spiritual wilderness. What we will have, instead, is a superficial *adaptation* of the gospel text to modern life, not an *inculturated* faith which our recent popes and religious leaders have called for. Christian imagination alone can render this task imaginable and achievable. If we are unable or unwilling to rely more heavily on our religious imagination – not only for our personal faith journey but also for the Church's mission in today's changing world – then we are sorely handicapped as we begin the new millennium.

Like Lazarus, there is every indication that the religious imagination is being given a new lease on life in recent times and is the object of increasing interest and research. The imagination is no longer viewed as a repository or storehouse of received images coming to it from the five senses. Nor is it simply viewed as one mental faculty or power among several others, operating pretty much independently of the others. It is a posture of the soul, a basic process which involves the whole person, intuition and wonder, but also the ability to see something good, something beautiful, even in the most unlikely people, places and happenings. Historians are now even proposing a new understanding and way of writing history, namely, the history of the imagination. As Jacques Le Goff puts it, "The history of the imagination is an elaboration of the history of conscience…. The imagination nourishes man and causes him to act. It is a collective, social and historical phenomenon. A history without the imagination is a mutilated, disembodied history. To study the imagination of a society is to go to the heart of its consciousness and historical evolution. It is to go to the origin and the profound nature of man, created 'in the image of God.'"[2]

Lazarus represents life and renewal – not death! In Chapter 1, with an example taken from my own personal history and the biographical reminiscences of my university graduate students, I endeavour to illustrate how the religious imagination actually functions in the lives of ordinary Christians. In Chapter 2, I highlight three areas in which religious imagination is sorely – at times abysmally – lacking in the Church today: in her liturgical performances, in her attempts to communicate deeply and meaningfully to the faithful, and in the area of what she has come to consider "sacred art." In Part II of this study, I have attempted to analyze and articulate the play, the gifts and the geographical "landscapes" of the religious imagination. In Part III, I make bold to suggest some signs which would seem to indicate that Lazarus may be "coming out" of his tomb and that Christians today are beginning, as in centuries past and however tentatively, to re-appropriate their religious imagination.

Before we begin, a word of caution. The imagination is not in the business of making predictions about the future – and certainly not à-la-Nostradamus or even à-la-Toffler. The imagination does not make predictions *about* the future – indeed has no need to! – for the simple reason that it *creates* the future. What the imagination does, and does very well, is make us creatively forge ahead into the future, knowing, as we do, that there is no road or path in front of us, especially in a desert wilderness.

Part I

The Village of Bethany Revisited

There was a man named Lazarus

in the village of Bethany

− and he was ill.

John 11:1

(Jerusalem Bible)

1

When You Think of God,
What Do You See?

I was challenged to look at my image of God
to test how closely it reflects that of Jesus,
how it compares with that of
my church and my culture.
— Karen Neuser

Perhaps the best way to introduce the perspective I am attempting to develop is to begin with a personal story, an account of my first childhood experience of being "taken in" one day
by my mother's Christian imagination and how this was to influence
my subsequent life of faith. I was only five or six years old when I
first became aware that my mother had been making repeated
mention of a place called Heaven, particularly on those occasions
when she had to reprimand me for teasing my brothers and sisters.

I was a big teaser in the eyes of my siblings and had earned the family nickname "the little devil." At first, I didn't take my mother's "heavenly" admonitions too seriously: they were, I devilishly assumed, but the clever ploy most mothers use at one time or another to get their children to behave. We were made to believe that Heaven was a good place to be, and – if one wasn't there yet – it was surely the place one was expected to prepare and long for.

Restless and always anxious for something better than the life my six brothers and sisters and I knew, growing up in the years following the Great Depression, I asked my mother one day – quite out of the blue – where this place called "Heaven" was and what it was like. Having been educated in a private Catholic school run by nuns in Salem, Massachusetts, my mother had learned her catechism well and knew most of the answers by heart. She may have sensed that my question was innocent enough and might provide a good "teaching moment," as we would say today, or she may have thought, not unreasonably, that her "little devil" was putting her to yet another test. In any event, I remember she stopped doing the dishes, turned and looked straight at me and in a measured tone of voice, said, "Heaven, Dickie, is where we'll all go one day when we die – if, in this life, we really love and serve God with all our heart."

"What will we do there?" I pursued, taking little notice of her conditional qualifier.

"We'll be with God for all eternity," she said, "and we'll get to see Him face to face. Won't that be nice?"

"You mean that's all?" I replied, no doubt registering that transparent look of an innocent child when deep disappointment begins to set in. "You mean that's it?... Just looking at God all the time, with nothing else to do?"

The sudden prospect of such a boring afterlife was especially dismal for me since I was always a somewhat restless and adventurous lad. So great was my letdown, in fact, that to this day, I still recall this being my first close encounter with the *real* devil, that is, with my first temptation to dismiss God as a "bad joke." At least the pranks I used to play on my brothers and sisters were *good* jokes – or so they seemed to me. What made this temptation seem very real to me was certainly related to those boring Sunday-afternoon visits my family occasionally made to our aunt and uncle who lived, as we used to say, "up on the hill." Like the God we imagined and prayed to as children, my aunt and uncle actually did live on a big hill – a hill that seemed enormous in those early days of our childhood. Upon arriving at their big white house overlooking the valley below and before getting out of the car, we would invariably be admonished, "Now you kids be good! Just sit and listen! And don't go running around the house or touch anything. Do you hear? You know how your Aunt Mary doesn't like to have anyone touch or play with her things."

So for what seemed to us an eternity – the same kind of "forever and ever" I remember experiencing at church on Sunday when Father O'Connor, our pastor, was saying Mass and preaching – we dutifully spent the afternoon sitting bolt upright on Aunt Mary's kitchen chairs, in fidgety silence, just looking around as the elders engaged in a conversation we neither followed nor understood. We were careful, moreover, to speak only when spoken to. Those were the days when, on such occasions, children were to be seen and not heard!

My mother had indeed impressed upon us that Heaven was like a big family gathering where most of us good Catholics would be reunited (this was before we allowed Protestants to sit in with us!). Still, the prospect of just "sitting still" and looking at God for all eternity disappointed me, even though we were to see him "up close" like Mother said.

My disappointment, however, did not go unnoticed for long. After a thoughtful pause, my mother dried her hands and took up the conversation again. "Let me put it this way, Dickie," she began, creating her own parable of what Heaven might be like. "Heaven's a wonderful place! Whenever we want something in this life and, for whatever reason, can't get or have it, God will see to it that all our wishes and desires are fulfilled in Heaven."

"You mean if you and Papa never get enough money to buy me a bicycle," I said, "God will make sure that I have one in Heaven?"

"That's right," she replied, "but you must wish for it *real hard!* You *really* have to want it badly! Otherwise God will not take you seriously."

"What if I'd like to become a pilot or a priest when I grow up, but something happens or goes wrong? Does that mean I can fly a plane or say Mass in Heaven?"

"Only if that's what you really want," she insisted again. "It must be something you want more than anything else in the world."

She gave me time to think this over and returned to the dishes. After a few moments of silence, I continued, "Mama, why do we always seem to need or want so many things? Is it because we're poor and can't afford it – like Papa keeps telling us?"

"No!" she said. "All our dreams and desires come from God. They belong to him. He just gives them to us to see how many we can fulfill in this life. Those we can't, God will make up in Heaven."

Convinced that the degree of joy and happiness we were to experience in Heaven was somehow in direct proportion to the number of unfulfilled desires we might experience in *this* life, I set out, quite deliberately, to conjure up as many "urgent longings" as my heart would allow. In time, this would become for me an exercise that took on the glow of a medieval mystery play or the comparable staging of the shadow play between the real and the imaginary. These longings included, I remember well, an ardent desire to become a renowned tenor, like Mario Lanza, whose songs I used to try to sing in the big hallway of our old farmhouse (much to the chagrin of my brothers and sisters who had to endure my attempts to reach high C); to become the operator of a big yellow crane that could lift and move the heaviest of objects; to become a priest who could "outshine" Fr. O'Connor and get all that money from the Sunday collection that mysteriously disappeared into the sacristy when the Mass was over; and to become a rich landowner one day, with a big white house "on a hill" like my Uncle Edmond. In my considerably active imagination, I entertained these and other youthful scenarios as though my eternal destiny somehow depended on the sincerity and intensity of my desires. Even though, deep down in my heart, I knew that none of these scenarios fell even remotely within the realm of possibility, I nevertheless remember *living* them with all the innocence of a child trying to be good while awaiting the coming of Santa Claus. That these urgent longings were unattainable seems not to have deterred me in the least. If my mother was right, I was at least certain that *my* Heaven would not be a boring place, however long it lasted and whatever it was we might do there.

It was only years later that I came to appreciate more fully the primal mystical wisdom in these childhood musings and the providential role they were to play in my subsequent faith journey. What I now realize is just how deeply rooted our prevailing image of God is in our actual experience of life. The interface between what we personally experience in life and the potent images of God we create for ourselves is quite remarkable. Since there seemed to be no earthly end to the wild scenarios I could dream up as a child, I quite spontaneously came to think of God as being somewhat wild and extravagant. If my own listening heart and imagination could run wild, then how much more extravagant must be God's imagination – he who creates and lends us all our earthly desires in the first place! And since my imaginative scenarios were all viscerally important to me, all equally attractive, all beautiful and capable of making me happy, I naturally assumed that God, too, must be extremely happy since he could not possibly want for anything. This was my first youthful intimation that God and we humans really do have something in common, a certain unspoken but real affinity between us, namely, the ability to "dream dreams" of what might be and the sheer joy and happiness of anticipating a day when these "impossible" dreams might became a reality. In short, I reckoned that even God must be anticipating a happy future – like me. Since I was convinced that most of my urgent longings would never be fulfilled in this life, but ultimately depended on his promise to "make good," I knew then, even though dimly, that our two destinies were somehow inexorably linked and that nothing on earth could ever separate or seriously come between us. To the best of my recollection, this was the first time that the God of my early childhood became real for me. Years later in the seminary, when I first came across St. Augustine's profound words – "Our hearts are restless until they rest in Thee, O Lord" – I had the distinct impression that Augustine simply put into fancier words what my mother had told me years earlier.

This was the way I imagined God in early childhood: wild, extravagant, seductive and happy-go-lucky. And imagining these characteristics about God put a real, honest-to-goodness "face" on

God…a face not altogether unlike my own. This was a God after my own heart, it seemed to me, created in my very own image and likeness, or was it the other way around? The question of who "imaged" whom obviously never occurred to me then, nor does it much matter even today. What fired my imagination and fuelled my early religious sensibility was the thought that God was not indifferent to what I was experiencing in my heart and in my life. And with that understanding, my dream of becoming a missionary priest gradually became ever more persistent. I remember making a little altar and "playing" Mass, with all my brothers and sisters dutifully receiving the small pieces of crushed white bread that I gave out to them at Communion. It was as though the words of Jonathan's young armour-bearer became increasingly my own: "Do just as your heart tells you; as for me, my heart is with you" (1 Samuel 14:7; Jerusalem Bible).

The memory of this early active imagination never seems to have left me; I look upon it even now as a precious "peak" religious experience of my early childhood. I call it a peak experience because it is still vividly etched in my memory and has always been a source of inspiration and direction in my faith journey to this very day. From our earliest childhood to our dying days, our faith requires an active dialogue with promise. Not just any kind of promise, but one that nourishes and makes explicit appeals to one's religious imagination – that faculty which alone is capable of forever evoking in us new mobilizing images of the face of God. It is for lack of such direct appeals to the Christian imagination, I will argue in this study, that so many Catholics currently find that their faith has become dysfunctional in the modern world and quite unrelated to their everyday preoccupations and concerns.

Convinced that faith without imagination invariably ends up being a *listless* faith, that is, a faith not fully experienced or lived out, I decided three years ago to explore with my students the connection between faith and the play of imagination. I introduced a new course in our graduate Mission Studies program at Saint Paul University, where I was lecturing, entitled "Faith and Imagination." To my surprise, the course attracted more students than I had anticipated. Some of them, I later learned, opted for this course out of intellectual curiosity; others, because they felt something vital was missing in their theological studies; and a few, because they were already actively seeking "alternative ways" of being a Christian in today's world. The latter students were the ones who came already convinced of the imagination's creative possibilities and its crucial role for transcending – "going beyond" – rational concepts in order to mediate those experiences that defy conceptual analysis.

The first thing I did, after briefly introducing myself and the course outline, was to assign my students a 25-page written "autobiography," not of their life history in the usual sense but an autobiography of their religious imagination. Rather than asking them to focus on the outer events of their lives, I asked them to trace the path of their religious imagination and the struggles they may have experienced at some crucial points in their lives when they felt summoned from within to "go beyond" their previously held images of God: that is to say, I explained to them, the history of those special moments of grace in their lives when something "sacred," however defined, quite unexpectedly captivated and fuelled their religious imagination. Could they identify and revisit these sacred moments in their faith journey as far back as they could remember? I invited them to linger long enough in these religious landscapes of their past to recapture something of the image of God that had inhabited them at the time, along with all the personal feelings, emotions and intuitions associated with this image.

My purpose in giving this assignment was to have the students reconstruct, as faithfully as possible, a composite picture, or profile, of their spiritual odyssey, the way their image of God had changed at various stages in their lives, and what perhaps prompted them to make these changes. The idea was to enable them, perhaps for the first time, to retrace the history of their *active* religious imagination, its play and sequential evolution in their life of faith, and how this correlated with their ongoing experience of the presence and/or absence of God in their life of faith. While respecting the confidentiality of these personal journals, I am going to highlight some of the general findings and salient points that emerged from this rewarding exercise.

Holding On and Letting Go

The first thing this exercise did was to clarify and confirm my own working assumption that the play of imagination is not merely an incidental or fortuitous occurrence in our life of faith but, rather, an abiding, constitutive element of faith itself – indeed something without which faith in a living God can become dysfunctional. What emerged from this exercise was a strong conviction that imagination plays a much more crucial role in our life of faith than is generally acknowledged. In hindsight, the students came to realize that we all grow up in a sea of religious images of God and that the essence of one's faith journey consists in learning how to swim in that sea. With few exceptions, the students describe the story of their religious imagination as one of learning how to appropriate "received" images of God, of understanding these images, checking them out, seeing to what extent they are really anchored in their experience of life and of how God is mysteriously at work in their lives. This is what the whole "culture of religious imagination" is all about. What the students discovered is that we do indeed make sense of God only by creating images of him that are deeply rooted in our personal history, not necessarily those that are "handed down" to us by official church teaching and tradition.

The reason why this distinction is so very important is because images symbolize our experience. They capture the totality of our felt response to reality in a given situation. When we reflect upon our experience, we encounter a host of feelings, thoughts, attitudes and hopes that accompany us into and out of a given situation in life. And when we pay close attention to these feelings, an image spontaneously arises and captures the essence of our experience in its totality, puts it "in a nutshell," as it were, and thus enables us to appropriate and "own" the experience more fully. These images, in turn, shed new light on the meaning of our lives; they give us new insight, not only into the way we stand before others and before God, but also into new and possible ways of being-in-the-world. Their capacity to capture our attention and shed new meaning on a situation is what makes images so powerful, and what also explains why they can at times be so disconcerting.

In fact, what proved in many instances to be a very painful struggle for these students was precisely when they felt obliged to wrestle with and shed a particular image of God that they had "received" from their parents, teachers or pastors in favour of one they felt was more authentic. The crucial question then becomes knowing when to "hold on" and when to "let go," an issue that some developmental psychologists refer to as a "holding environment" and "transitional space." A holding environment is one in which we are comfortable with the temporary settings of our life of faith. We are content with the prevailing image of God that dwells in us, the one we spontaneously turn to when in doubt or in time of prayer, the image from which we draw direct spiritual benefit and which clings to us like a shadow. Transitional space, on the other hand, is a place of imbalance and discomfort, a time when we feel summoned to "let go" of something. Every student, without exception, spoke of one or more such "transitional spaces" in their life of faith.

When this shift happens, we feel that something is being taken away from us without our consent. Sharon Parks, following clinical psychologist and theologian James Loder, describes this first critical "moment" of conscious conflict that thrusts us out of a previous "holding environment" and into "transitional space":

> Conflict may be present in an unconscious or preconscious sense, but it does not become available for the re-composing of meaning and for the transformation of faith until it is brought to the conscious level. This may emerge as an increasing curiosity, a devastating shattering of assumptions, a vague restlessness, an intense weariness with things as they are, a body of broken expectations, an interpersonal conflict, or a discovery of intellectual dissonance. In this moment, equilibrium is thrown off balance.[3]

The conflict involved in transitional space is initially experienced as a "baffling struggle with irreconcilable factors."[4] As a result, we can no longer pray as we once did, attend church with the same devotion as before or experience the closeness of God's presence in the same way.

These transitional spaces in our life of faith can descend upon us either very dramatically or in a subtle, almost imperceptible fashion: dramatically, as, for instance, when we are suddenly diagnosed with a terminal illness, or face the prospect of surgery or the trauma of a car accident in which someone is killed; or, imperceptibly, as when we experience a prolonged sense of boredom or ennui in life, the onset of a mid-life crisis, or simply the aging process that sorely reminds us that we can no longer do – or do as well – many of the things we once did. If we are to successfully negotiate transitional space in terms of *real* spiritual growth and development, we must allow our imagination considerable freedom to entertain alternative ways of re-visioning and re-assembling all the aspects of the conflict. Only then can we hope to gain a new vision of reality. This is where the vitalizing power of imagination becomes most crucial. Either we grant it permission to give new form to our faith or we exclude it at considerable spiritual loss.

The imagination looks favourably upon these periods of disequilibrium and imbalance; it sees in them a "blessing in disguise," as it were, an opportunity to come alive to new visions and new possibilities. In the words of Horace Bushnell, it is "the soul struggling to utter itself." In the words of the New Testament, it is "the assurance of things hoped for, the conviction of things not seen" (Hebrews 11:1). This is when the Christian imagination becomes most creative and summons us to new and deeper insight. It is a time and season when the creative power of the Spirit is most available to us.

What became clear to the students in their subsequent "imaginal" encounters with God was the extent to which their religious imagination was both receptive and constructive, that is, how deeply embedded it was within, but not imprisoned by, the Church's official teaching or tradition. It also became clear that their Christian imagination was profoundly shaped by the socio-historical context of their lives; the geographical landscapes in which they lived; the family settings in which they grew up; and the overall *pattern* of their thoughts, feelings, impressions and intuitions which prevailed at a given time in their lives.

The interesting thing, too, is that the more these students were able to trace and reconstruct the actual path along which their religious imagination had taken them over the years, the more they came to realize the providential role of images in their spiritual journey: how any given image of God can, and often does, provoke a subtle or profound transformation in their being and actions. In virtually every case, it was the inadequacy of a certain previously held image of God that occasioned and triggered a conscious decision to "move on" – some away from religious practice, others to the arduous task of "reconstructing" for themselves a new and perhaps more congenial image of God. The students described how it was their prevailing, taken-for-granted image of God that "occasioned," "prompted" or otherwise "precipitated" a reassessment of their faith commitment, at times with considerable soul-searching and anxiety. Without a commitment to question and reassess their image of God, it seemed to them, their faith in God and religion became increasingly problematic, and they could not see how God could "fit" into or occupy a significant place in their personal experience of life. Thus the proverbial "shoe" began to pinch! What they were saying, in effect, was that they did not just wake up one fine morning and resolve to take their faith more seriously, or less seriously. Rather, it was just the opposite: it was the particular image of God that "inhabited" them which became problematic and, over time, no longer seemed credible in its present configuration. As they became increasingly aware of this, some more quickly than others, a revision of some sort was needed.

The Many Faces of God

A second remarkable thing about the students' assignment was the astonishing variety of images of God which had been or were being entertained. What I found particularly interesting was the way they looked back upon, and *now* viewed and considered, their early childhood images of God. It seems that how one *begins* to image God in early childhood already tells us something about the way we eventually come to envisage God later in life. It is as though no matter how much our conception of God is modified or changes over the years, in hindsight at least, we never seem to completely shed or lose our initial insight into the reality of God. Within our childhood images, as in embryonic or larval form, there lies "enfolded" the whole as yet unwritten story of our subsequent faith journey, however tortuous or hesitant this journey may be. It is as though our first image of God carries with it a crucial invitation from God that continues to emerge, time and time again, in our faith journey, albeit in different ways. Hence the importance of revisiting and getting "in touch" with these earlier impressions and images of God. They are full of meaning and shed considerable light on our subsequent journey in faith.

For many students, it was a particular religious *object* or *thing* that first captured their baptismal imagination, that gave imaginal form to their first experience of God. It may have been a religious object: a picture of the Sacred Heart, for instance, pierced by a sword and bleeding profusely; a veiled tabernacle under lock and key on the altar; the smell of incense; the congenial touch of holy water or the foreboding black colour of the pastor's cassock; the sound of their mother's voice at bedtime, "Don't forget to say your prayers"; their first encounter with a question in the Church's catechism such as "Where is God?" and the answer: "God is everywhere." For others, it was not a religious object or person at all, but simply an ordinary, everyday thing that gradually took on a sacred quality all its own. It could be a particular tree in whose branches the child loves to climb to experience the thrill of being elevated on high or the thrill of being alone and quite on their own. It could be something as simple as a favourite mound of earth or rock on which a child loves to play and actively imagine what it must be like to be an adult; or a cuddly teddy bear, with whom the child can share its most intimate thoughts and secrets. For others, it might be a special person who suddenly steps into their life, unannounced and ever so briefly, and who impresses them deeply with just a simple word, an affectionate gesture or smile, as if letting them "in" on some big secret or mystery.

What is noteworthy about all such early moments of grace is that they are frequently *ambiguous*. Our first impressions of God can please and disturb us, satisfy and startle us, all at once. By so doing, they command our attention and prod us to ponder and muse on the image, wondering what it means and where it might take us. Moreover, what may prove to be an initial positive experience for one can be a negative experience for another. For example, a picture depicting a transfixed and bleeding Sacred Heart might be quite disgusting and even repulsive to one child, while evoking a deep sense of compassion in another. Or, again, the thought that "God is everywhere" may offer deep comfort and security to some, but to others it can instill the distinct feeling that, while unseen, God watches our every move like a "Big Spy" and carefully records our every secret thought. There is ample evidence in the students' autobiographies to confirm Rudolf Otto's famous contention that any close encounter with the "Holy" is both inviting and threatening, alluring and terrifying, all at once.

Thus our earliest image of God is rarely, if ever, one-dimensional. It is, rather, polyvalent. Our first glimpse of God's face is given to us like a "coat of many colours." At one and the same time, God may appear as *wonderful* (in the sense of evoking wonders that cause amazement), *awful* (in the sense of inspiring reverential fear), *terrible* (in the sense of awakening terror) or *overwhelming* (in the sense of being beyond one's control). In addition, a careful study of these early childhood "inscapes" of God reveals that what may initially start out as a comforting or liberating image can subsequently reverse itself, turn hostile or demonic and completely shatter the peaceful way in which we hitherto tried to "possess" our faith. Paradoxically, what may have begun as a positive image of God can become, over time, the very image that stunts our growth and development in the life of faith. It may also happen that an initial fear of God may subsequently give way to a most engaging, intimate relationship.

All this, of course, touches directly on the way the Holy Spirit moves so unpredictably and unobtrusively in our lives and our world. It also has tremendous pastoral implications for a Church whose life is pervasively steeped in sacred images, symbols and metaphors about God's kingdom. The important role of the religious imagination in the unfolding story of the Christian community, how it functions and the way it beckons us to follow Christ in ever-new creative ways of being present in the world will be the main focus of this study. Religious imagination also plays a crucial mediating role between what the Church officially teaches and the way this teaching is actually "received" by the faithful. A pastoral approach that ignores this mediating role does so at the risk of seeing church teaching go largely unheeded. We are forever being invited to go "behind" and "beyond" our accepted representations of God. Herein lies the unique power of the religious imagination: it entices us, if we are willing and ready, to re-vision our image of God. Many think of imagination as a dreamer's flight from reality, an untrustworthy guide, a passing illusion. In truth, however, imagination signifies something much more profound. As Leonardo Boff rightly puts it, "Imagination is a form of liberty." It allows the believer to see beyond what meets the eye, beyond the established order of things in our world today and to begin imagining what the kingdom of God is really like when it makes its appearance "in our very midst."

The Church seems to have underestimated the vital role that the Christian imagination actually plays in the religious life and behaviour of the faithful. Even in its own venerable historical tradition, there were times when the Church powerfully appealed to and engaged the religious imagination of the faithful. We see this, for example, in the way the Church captivated and fired the religious imaginations and hearts of the faithful in those truly great missionary epochs of the sixth, sixteenth and nineteenth centuries. Or, more recently, the way Good Pope John XXIII let loose and fired the creative imaginations of the faithful by calling for the Second Vatican Council. Much of the Church's own remarkable community-building power in the past was generated, to a large extent, by her numerous, generous and direct appeals to the Christian imagination of the faithful. The secret of the Church's evangelizing efforts and success, within as well as beyond her visible boundaries, has always depended on her ability to summon and call forth the religious imagination of the faithful. And in those times when this ability was lacking or found wanting in the Church, some individual, with considerable personal charisma, has risen up to inspire the faithful. Mother Teresa of Calcutta readily comes to mind, as do Archbishop Oscar Romero, Martin Luther King Jr., Pope John Paul II and many other singular individuals who have moved and shaped the Church of our times. The same could obviously be said of those numerous founders of religious congregations who, through a perceptive and imaginative reading of the "signs of the times," succeeded in attracting many vocations. Jesus himself was a person with an extraordinarily creative imagination;

whoever would follow him, even two thousand years later, must be prepared to use their religious imagination in order to remain faithful to him.

By Christian imagination, I mean that inherent baptismal endowment which alone enables the believer to think the unthinkable, to conceive the inconceivable and to imagine what can only be "imagined," namely, the coming of the kingdom of God in our very midst. Whenever we hear a word of hope or promise, we hear it, first and essentially, at the level of our imagination. This holds true for a human promise as well as a divine promise. And since the gospel is God's promise "made human," Christians of every age and century have always regarded their baptismal imagination as part and parcel of their life of faith, hope and charity. When this divine gift is stifled, repressed or not granted its rightful role in the life of the Christian community, religious belief all too readily becomes a purely rational ascent to credal truths instead of a relationship of deep trust and commitment. This reality became patently clear in the spiritual journals of my students. Even when frowned upon by their elders, they nevertheless felt summoned by their religious imagination to re-vision God in yet another way, one that would correlate more closely with what they were actually experiencing in life.

Admittedly, pursuing one's Christian imagination, like following one's conscience, can be unsettling and fraught with dangers. Unsettling because it may require that we give up one of our long-held images of God, and fraught with danger because religious imagination makes no claims to being infallible. Yet the fear of *not* taking this risk is equally perilous in terms of authentic spiritual growth and development. Nor should we be blind to the fact that the many who do accept this challenge, such as the great saints and mystics throughout history, often demonstrated more trust in God than was even acknowledged or recognized in their own lifetimes. The rejection of a limited or inadequate notion of God should not therefore be equated with religious apathy or indifference. I am reminded of that insightful little book written some years ago by J.B. Phillips, aptly titled *Your God Is Too Small*, in which the author exposes some of the inadequate conceptions of God which still linger unconsciously in many minds today, and which prevent us from catching a better glimpse of the true God. In a more recent and challenging book, *The God We Never Knew*, Marcus J. Borg traces the spiritual journey many take from outmoded childhood images of God to a more powerful, dynamic adult understanding of God.[5] Such a journey is, of course, less predictable and certainly more arduous than merely accepting, in blind obedience and without questioning, certain images of God. Hence the tendency to either cling to our traditional images of God or to recognize that perhaps our conceptions of God may indeed be too small, too inadequate or simply too removed from our present-day experience of life to be meaningful any longer.

Transforming Landscapes

A third salient feature in the students' assignment is the way their religious imagination gradually enticed them *away from a precise and more discrete image of God to one shrouded in greater mystery.* This change took place in virtually every account. For some, the shift was slow, gradual and scarcely remarkable; many were even unaware that such a transformation was taking place in their spiritual landscape until they had retraced the sequence of their prevailing images of God. For others, the transformation was more abrupt and memorable, often taking place in the wake of either a personal crisis or some unexpected turn of events in their lives.

This is particularly revealing because it tells us much about the way our faithful religious imagination "works," the spiritual path along which it would have us travel and just where this "kindly light" might take us on our faith journey. The road "less travelled" here is the very one the students discovered when recreating the history of their religious imagination. They found that, by and large, their early perceptions of God were more "precise," more "graphic," more in the nature of a vivid and clearly etched "picture." Like their sense of the sacred, their first images of God were sharper, more discrete or, as one of them put it, "more solid, less diffused." In time, however, and with the benefit of more experience, their perception of God became more ethereal, airy, light, almost "formless" – which is not to say that God had become "less real" for them, but only "less concrete." They came to realize how their religious imagination had gradually led them away from an overly "solid" image of God to images that were more vaporous and diffused.

With these more expansive, less material images of God, the students noted that they were now better able to experience the presence of God outside and beyond the specifically designated "sacred times" (like Sunday) and "sacred places" (like a church). They came to imagine God more as an "all-embracing" presence, the "ground" or "mystery" that somehow renders every thing and every being holy. In short, these more diffused images, metaphors and notions of God enabled them, they said, to "see" a reflection of God in the "everyday" sights and sounds of their otherwise quite ordinary workweek. They were now able to envisage God's presence in a beautiful sunset, a rolling hillside in autumn, a tiny raindrop, the cry of a newborn infant, the sight of a derelict streetwalker, the beat of heavy rock music or the sound of a tenor saxophone, a ghostly tree on a windy night or the warm embrace of a dear friend. As one of my students put it, "God is as colourful as he is colourless, pungent as he is bland. He is laughter in his silence and sings in the night."

What all this suggests, for those who allow their religious imagination some scope and freedom, is that the sharply drawn distinction between the "sacred" and the "profane" begins to disappear. Or should we not perhaps more appropriately say that, at last, the sacred and the profane begin to co-penetrate as in a nuptial union, much the same way that the divine and the human become one in the Incarnation of the Son of God. For my students, there no longer seemed to be such a divide or divorce between their "religious" life and their "everyday" life. With this heightened sense of integration in their personal life of faith, some students acknowledged experiencing alienation from their Church and earlier religious practice, while others felt more "at home" in the Church than ever before. In either case, however, both regarded their imaginal "conversion" as a blessing in disguise. In hindsight, they were now prepared to concede, as all the great saints and mystics have done in the past, that no one image can adequately express or represent the God of Jesus Christ.

Such personal stories, I am now convinced, are not as rare or exceptional in the lives of ordinary Christians as I once believed.

Nor are they to be viewed necessarily as a loss of faith in a *personal* God. Perhaps an analogy will help explain what I mean. There are a number of known physical elements in nature that can change from one form to another without changing their chemical nature, such as water in the form of a solid (ice), a liquid (water) or a vapour (mist). Similarly, our different perceptions of God may well be sharply defined and "solid" when we are young, only to become more vaporous and diffused as we grow in our life of faith. As infants in the life of faith, we rely more heavily on the religious imagination to produce vivid images of God. Later in life, our baptismal imagination progressively weans us off these more bold images of God in favour of more mystical ones. Our perception of God becomes less tangible, shrouded in greater ambiguity and mystery. When this happens, we come to "know" God differently; our knowledge of God becomes more humble, less sure of itself. And when this takes place, we begin to experience the "dark night" of the senses about which many great mystics speak.

The psalmist enjoins us to "Seek his face always" (Psalm 104:4). In this regard, our religious imagination is forever restless; it continually beckons and prompts us to seek an evermore authentic likeness of God for our day, even when we think we have found him. Whenever we become overly confident and secure in our image of God, our tendency is not unlike that of Peter, John and James when they saw Jesus transfigured on the mountain: we want to set up a tent and enjoy this experience as long as possible. But as Jesus reminded his disciples, this was not to be. Our religious imagination, quietly or disturbingly, prods us to search for yet another glimpse of his face. Sooner or later, our "holding" image of God seems to combust and, with it, comes the wrenching need to "let go" of our previously held image of God in favour of another. Someone once said that "To live is to change, and to become perfect is to have changed often." If this is true, then the many changes in our perception of God should come as no surprise. What *is* surprising is that, over time, these images tend to become more ill-defined and indeterminate. Instead of King, Lord or Father, for example, God is envisioned as Source of Life, Ultimate Reality or Ground of Being.

Many will deplore this transformation. Some will no doubt see this kind of transformation as but another sign that our modern society has depersonalized the God of biblical revelation. But this needn't be so. After all, what do we mean by a "personal" God? Is this not an anthropocentric way of speaking about God? Yes, from a very early age we were taught that God is personal. But in a sense God goes beyond the personal (as we know it), as he goes beyond every human category, including gender and even existence. While to speak of a personal God may be reassuring from our human point of view, and may even be our most humanly sublime way of envisioning God, does it not remain, for all that, a limited human analogy? Do we not feel, at times, as though there is in God something even greater and more profound, something that surpasses our human capacity to articulate or utter? Certainly, many of the great mystics thought so, as when they speak of a "dark night" of the senses or when they opt for a "negative" theology or a more "unknowing" (*apophatic*) approach to God. As Karl Rahner reminds us, even when we behold God in the beatific vision, our eternal bliss will consist precisely in the fact that he remains Mystery, that is, positively and supremely *Other.*

What we need, I am suggesting, is to recapture something of our lost mystical imagination: hence the title of this study, *Lazarus! Come Out!* The more attuned we become to the mysterious ways in which God works in our lives, and the more we begin to envision the Holy Spirit as God's own divine imagination working within us, the more we may come to appreciate the God of Jesus Christ, a God of pure *gratuitousness,* a God whose love for us knows absolutely no bounds, no limits and has no strings attached! For most of us, such a "wild" image of God does not readily enter our religious sensibility. The reason, I suspect, is because our Christian upbringing has conditioned us to think of God as one who exacts something in return for his bountiful, redeeming love, and who puts a premium on and reckons with our human efforts to remain in his "good grace." The tacit assumption here is that were God to dispense his divine grace too freely, too lavishly and too liberally – with absolutely no strings attached – this would depreciate and somehow "devalue" his love.

Thus many of our images of God tend to be self-centred and self-serving. We tend to think of God primarily in terms of what he has done and continues to do *for us and our salvation*, little else. In my youth, for example, I perceived God as being "good" and "loving" because I felt that he would answer *my* prayers, fulfill *my* dreams, satisfy *my* urgent longings. The measure of God's goodness and divine self-communication was defined only in terms of what I needed and desired most. It never occurred to me that I was perceiving God primarily as what the ancients would have called a "useful good" (*bonum utile*), as distinct from an "honest-to-goodness good" (*bonum honestum*), that is, something good in and of itself. Is God good and beautiful *only* because he redeems me and answers my prayers, or is he perhaps supremely beautiful and good *in himself,* regardless of how "useful" he may otherwise be for my personal salvation? Beautiful and good, that is, in and for himself alone? The necessity of God is very feeble if it is understood merely on the level of "utility." Extravagant as my youthful desires may have been, I can now dimly appreciate that God's goodness and beauty far surpass any and all of my most personal needs or urgent human longings. It took years for my Christian imagination to eventually wean me off an overly "utilitarian" image of God to one that affords me greater insight into the unimaginable beauty and goodness of God in his own divine being. Such an experience must have been Jesus' habitual way of looking upon his God, his "Abba."

The Gospel of John says that "God is love." Another John, the poet John Donne, says that "love is wild." When these two utterances are conjoined, as the best Christian tradition would have it, nothing can be ruled out of court. The utter gratuitous nature of God's total self-communication in Jesus Christ is such that it renders everything else in biblical revelation of secondary importance. God's gratuitousness is something literally and figuratively "out of this world!" (as the expression has it), something even beyond our human ability to name or articulate, beyond even our wildest musings and dreams. Our baptismal imagination is what gives us the courage to experience this daring "leap" into transcendence. The great St. Teresa of Avila certainly had it right when she said, "Never put a limit on God's love. He will not allow it."

2

The Demise of Lazarus

"Lord, he whom you love is ill."
– John 11:3

It is at the level of imagination that
contemporary Christianity is most weak.
– Dennis Nineham

Imagination is something that few people would readily admit to being totally without. At the same time, we are generally more prepared to recognize it in others than claim it for ourselves. In the preceding chapter, I have attempted to show that we all have much more imagination than we realize, and that our life of faith sorely depends on it. It is only a mild exaggeration (if that!) to say that without imagination, our Christian faith is in danger of becoming as lifeless as poor Lazarus entombed in his shroud. I have also shown that whenever we think of God, our imagination comes forcefully into play and not infrequently shatters our previously held notions and images. This brings us to the question of the apparent demise of imagination in the Church today. The failure or reluctance of the Church to appeal in a sustained manner to the Christian imagination of the faithful is seen by many as a crucial difficulty that many Catholics face. Here we will examine three significant areas in the present-day life of the Church where an appeal to the religious imagination of the faithful is conspicuously lacking. The reader is hereby forewarned: if the present chapter is more mournful in tone than the preceding one, the reader will at least be reminded of the loss that Jesus experienced at the untimely demise of his beloved friend Lazarus. John's Gospel records tersely, "Jesus began to weep" (John 11:35).

Unlike in past centuries, when popular piety and devotion thrived on religious imagination and indeed were sanctioned and encouraged by the Church, little concerted effort is made in the Church today to evoke and appeal to the religious imagination of the faithful. Like Lazarus, religious imagination seems to have been "put on hold." There was a time, of course, when Pope John XXIII and his Council did indeed fire the imagination of Christians around the world. The new windows that were then opened in the Church set free the religious imagination of bishops and laity alike and with this, a new way of *being* Church in the modern world emerged. Today, this singular event seems like ancient history – or so it now appears to anyone under 50 years of age. Those under 50 will have little way of knowing the exhilarating and creative release of Catholic imagination that took place at that time. When Pope John convened the Vatican Council, he allowed us to begin imagining what was hitherto unimaginable: a different Church, a different liturgy, a different way of imagining God and viewing the secular world, and a different way of relating to other world religions.

As we enter the third millennium, church leaders seem to have made a steady and concerted effort to put the proverbial lid back on Pandora's box, to rein in the seemingly out-of-control Catholic imagination. The many who initially attempted to keep Pandora's box open find themselves increasingly marginalized and under pressure to curb their religious and theological imagination. Church policy in the last two decades has clearly shifted from creative exploration to conformity, from a healthy acceptance of religious imagination to the restoration of doctrinal orthodoxy. But perhaps not entirely!

With his frequent travels throughout the world and bold utterances on peace and social justice, Pope John Paul II, in his own quite remarkable way and person, has at least kept the flame of Christian imagination alive in the world, if not always in his Church, and he has done this, moreover, as few other world leaders have. History may well record that Pope John Paul II, through the remarkable force of his personality and moral authority, has given the world sufficient imagination to dream new dreams and see new visions. Within the Church, however, he has allowed relatively fewer dreams or visions to emerge. Open to change for those outside the Church, he has frowned upon change within the Church. With an unimaginative Roman Curia, church affairs have been conducted after the model of rule by an absolute monarch. "We have a reformed Church and an unreformed papacy," as one respected journalist put it.

Yet this paradox is one that the Catholic imagination has come to accept and live with, especially at the grassroots level of the Church. On his tireless pilgrimages around the world, John Paul II has continued to amaze us and give us much to think about. Who could fail to be impressed by the way he has mobilized and captured the hearts of young people today, as few church leaders have, especially with his enthusiastic and most extravagant World Youth Days? And who can forget his historic visit to the Holy Land, which was, he said, one of his long-standing personal dreams? Given the highly charged political and religious situation in the Middle East, it could be argued that the pope's Jubilee Pilgrimage was the crowning glory and the most symbolic gesture of his pontificate. Its symbolic power was certainly not lost on anyone among the three Abrahamic faiths (Judaism, Christianity and Islam). Living symbols such as these are precisely what quickens the religious imagination of the faithful, much more than any spoken word or papal teaching.

Instead of regarding herself as a buttressed institution, solidly grounded on the shore of orthodoxy and conformity, the Church does well to take the risk of boldly launching out into the deep, like St. Peter, to meet the Lord walking on the uncertain waters of our contemporary times and sensibilities. In order to do this as her essential vocation, both "in season and out of season," the Church must find a way to resuscitate and enlist the baptized imagination of the faithful. Without it – again like St. Peter – she may well hesitate and will almost certainly flounder. The rest of this study will attempt to validate this claim and show why it cannot be otherwise. In this chapter, I merely wish to signal three vital areas where the absence of religious imagination in the Church today is most conspicuous and regretful.

The Liturgical Scene

One of the more obvious places where religious imagination is lacking is in the Church's liturgy in general and in the eucharistic celebration in particular. This is most unfortunate because it is during Sunday Mass that the Church is assembled as a faith community on a regular basis, all over the world – from the most remote mountain villages to the most populated cities. At no other time does the Church's liturgy and ritual "hit the road" more frequently and engage more Catholics in its pastoral ministry and devotional resolve than on these weekly occasions. And yet, there is little in the way the Eucharist is celebrated today that evokes or makes an unequivocal appeal to the religious imagination of the faithful. Although it is replete with symbols, ritual action, liturgical gestures and gospel narratives, the celebration itself all too frequently remains but a rational, perfunctory exercise. Clearly, one of the major reasons is that everything is explained, interpreted, made explicit and "understandable" in the Mass. Nothing is left to the imagination – as though the primary purpose of the liturgy and the gospel stories is to provide an occasion and raw material for catechetical explanation and moral reflection. Liturgical symbols are approached rationally, not imaginatively, and so they fall silent, like Lazarus in his tomb, no longer able to function and do for us what only *living* symbols are able to do when we respect and allow them to function symbolically. Rarely do the symbols embodied in the eucharistic rite surprise the faithful or move them to awe and wonder; rarely do they touch the faithful *beyond* what superficially meets the eye or the ear, beyond what humanly can be understood or grasped. It is as though our liturgical symbols have lost their power to mobilize the Christian community. Why is this? Why have so many of our traditional Christian symbols fallen "silent"?

The trouble is not so much that the faithful have lost their sense of mystery or their capacity to be moved and seduced by real living symbols. My contention is, rather, that present-day liturgists and presiders of the liturgy seem to have scant knowledge of the way symbols are to be respected in a ritual setting or how they are meant to seduce us, rather than be explained to us. As a result, the religious imagination of the faithful – like the automobile they came to church in – is left outside in the parking lot, "out in the cold," as it were. Andrew Greeley puts it this way: "They [the faithful] may believe intellectually that they have participated in a love feast, but the event fails to communicate such a story to their imagination."[6]

One of the reasons there is so little room for imagination in today's liturgy is because our religious symbols are too often treated as signs. The difference between a *sign* and a *symbol* is noteworthy. A sign is a reference to something that is known or knowable in a perfectly rational way. For instance, when you come across a road sign that reads "To Montreal," the sign "stands for" a knowable, physical place. But a symbol does not refer to something that is known or knowable in that way. It refers to a spiritual power that is released from *within* the symbol, quite apart from what we may or may not know or understand. This is precisely what gives symbols their uncanny power to entice and seduce, as when my mother captivated me as a child with her symbolic interpretation of heaven. The secret here is to give the symbol sufficient permission and ritual space to cast its spell over our religious imagination and thus produce its powerful effects in us. We should try not to "grasp" or rationally take hold of a symbol, as so many liturgical presiders would have us do; rather, it is the symbol, with its own inherent power of seduction, that should come to meet and "take possession" of us. In other words, good liturgy is all about *being seduced* by the power of living symbols.

What exactly is this strange power? How do symbols seduce, mobilize and transform us? First, a symbol will seek to eliminate or neutralize those excessive fears that can so easily impede our growth and further development such as the fear of death or fear of the unknown, those deep-seated human fears that can easily paralyze and prevent us from moving ahead in the face of life's risks and terrible dangers. Thus the symbol of a Creator God seeks to give us the assurance that we can and should, in all confidence, assume our fragile human condition and vulnerability without undue pessimism. As a symbol, the Creator God prevents us from falling into despair or cynicism. By removing our worst fears, symbols enable us to make the most of our potential, even when the odds are great and the future is bleak. In their own peculiar way, symbols give us the "courage to be" in a fragile and often violent world, the courage to accept human existence *as though* this were a divinely appointed vocation. From a Christian perspective, symbols reassure us that God did not make some big and terrible mistake when he created us and our world the way he did.

Second, a living symbol has the power to unite what we often experience or perceive as fragmentary, even contradictory, in our lives, our world and our community of faith. It pulls together the many conflicting impulses and "personalities" we experience, and brings about a greater sense of oneness and integrity of being. Symbols prevents us from becoming a dysfunctional, divided self or community. To prevent my experiencing life as an untidy clutter of disparate, often conflicting, impulses, symbols enable me to "possess my soul," as the ancients would say. And they do this by disclosing real, mysterious, in-depth connections between realities we generally tend to polarize as clear-cut opposites: sacred/profane, good/evil, order/disorder, fact/fantasy, control/freedom, positive/negative, *eros/agape*, mind/body, natural/supernatural, etc. Unlike our usual rational way of thinking, the symbolic imagination abhors any and all neat categories and clear-cut distinctions. And the reason is that every symbol, by its very nature, implies and does, in fact, contain its opposite – indeed, multiple opposites. Symbols are multi-faceted, charged with the potential of evoking a host of diverse, even contradictory, meanings. This is what gives symbols both their richness and their power: they never "mean" only one thing. Presiders at the liturgy often try to sanitize symbols by removing their inherent tensive polysemy. When they do this, by trying to "explain" the symbol in rational terms, they end up destroying the symbol and depriving the faithful of its real power to transform.

Third, symbols open up new levels of awareness about ourselves and about reality that would otherwise remain hidden were they not "insinuated" to us by the magic of symbols. They give us insight into the deeper, transcendent meaning of every created being, human and non-human. When a symbol loses its power to reveal something *new* to us, something we perhaps never conceived of before, then it has obviously failed to initiate us deeper into the liturgical mysteries we celebrate.

Fourth, living symbols have great mobilizing power. When properly handled and respected, they can elicit a potential in us to commit ourselves in ways we didn't know we were capable of. They set us free, individually and as a community, to undertake great, even heroic, achievements in life. They give sinners the incentive to become holy, the holy to become saints, the saints to become heroic. In short, they give us the courage to dare to do the impossible and the audacity to go out on the proverbial limb in self-sacrifice for others. They give us the necessary incentive to pursue those arduous tasks in life that we would otherwise prefer to shun. If there is one virtue, in particular, that symbols seek to instill in us, it is the virtue of magnanimity.

Briefly, these are what our sacred symbols can do for us if we respect and celebrate them properly. Yet for all their power and saving grace, the effectiveness of these symbols depends on whether or not in the liturgical rite the religious imagination of the faithful is enlisted and granted unfettered access. Roger Haight, who has taught at Weston Jesuit School of Theology in Cambridge since 1990, makes the point well:

> Many theologians correctly see a close relation between faith and the power of imagination. Symbols too are *obviously* linked to the imagination. By mediating to consciousness the object of faith, symbols release the imagination as the power of the mind to construe reality in dimensions that far exceed their empirical appearance. The imagination, by projecting and injecting deeper meaning into reality, also discovers dimensions that are already there.... In sum, symbols bestow meaning on the external world by allowing human beings to see with their imagination what would otherwise remain hidden.[7]

An example may help to illustrate this more concretely. Everyone is familiar with the parable of the prodigal son. A literal reading or interpretation of this story simply reduces it to an edifying moral story or lesson. A symbolic encounter with this parable is something quite different. In this parable there are three major characters: the compassionate father, the prodigal son and his elder brother. The three characters in this story are well-defined, distinct and unmistakable. If one interprets this parable literally, the three characters remain just that: three very distinct characters. If, however, this parable is received symbolically, as it should be and as a story that is *actually taking place within the soul of the listener*, then a new level of awareness is opened up. We suddenly have a "three-in-one" person, not three distinct characters. One of the salient features of every symbol is to unite rather than distinguish. Thus as a participant in this symbolic tale, I am suddenly made aware that there is in *me* something of the father's forgiving nature and unconditional love; something in *me*, also, that identifies with the prodigal son's more adventurous nature and his urgent need to see and experience the world "out there"; and finally, there is something in *me* of the elder brother who is duty-bound and envious of those who get something they don't deserve or haven't really earned. Thus instead of being simply a story with a moral lesson, the parable now becomes a powerful symbolic tale: it disturbs me profoundly, touches me deeply and prevents me from passing judgment on any one of the three characters. Instead, the symbol probes the unfolding drama within me, thus simultaneously implicating me in the fate and destiny of all three.

By holding all the elements of the story symbolically together, the creative tension between duty and freedom, justice and compassion, obedience and creativity, is maintained. The parable, then, *as symbol,* comes alive. That is to say, it can now dispel excessive fear, foster greater integration, disclose new meaning and mobilize further commitment.

One of the reasons why many older Catholics still yearn for the celebration of the old Tridentine Mass is that despite all its imperfections, this rite did exude a sense of mystery – something our modern celebration of the Eucharist dismally fails to achieve. For one thing, today's ritual includes far too many readings with the connection between them often being contrived and superficial. Another thing sorely missing in today's liturgy is "stillness" and moments of prolonged silence, without which the religious imagination is severely handicapped. In today's celebration of the Eucharist, we are made to sing, read, recite or listen to endless texts. And the few sporadic moments of silence that are interjected in the ritual we usually experience as an awkward, "hollow" time in the rite. I remember my sister, a devout Catholic and mother of six children, telling me one day after Mass that she could pray much better at home than at church. She felt that she was kept "too busy" at Mass to pray, there was just "too much going on." A ritual *is* dramatic action and, as such, does require active participation, but not to the exclusion of a sense of mystery and sufficient stillness for the play of imagination.

Good liturgy engages our imaginations to a point where the question of God and how we stand before him becomes inescapable. Liturgical utterances are not so much words of information, but words of insinuation and seduction. Liturgical gestures are not meant to entertain, illustrate or embellish a rite; they are meant to heal, mobilize and ultimately lead us deeper into the inexpressible mystery of our faith and our hope. Liturgists and celebrants render far too explicitly what should be left to the imagination of the faithful. They would do better to give the imagination of the faithful greater "permission" to experience and interpret the symbolic rite. The sacrament of the Eucharist, like any one of its many symbols, should be allowed – indeed strongly encouraged – to evoke and express as many meanings as are inherent in the rite. To make a symbol one-dimensional is to kill it. The Mass is indeed communion and table fellowship with the Lord. But it is not *only* that! The symbolism of the Eucharist is also sacrifice, mystery, prophecy, judgment, death, atonement, believing without seeing, life, reconciliation, resurrection.

What this means in practice is that the faithful should not be made to feel that there is only one way to approach the symbolic rite, or that they must encounter and be seduced by a symbol in one particular, pre-determined way. If presented properly, the symbol will seek out, find and seduce the faithful in as many different ways as there are participants, provided the celebrant allows ample room in the rite for the play of the faithful's religious imagination. Living symbols come to meet and seduce us, often when we least expect it. This is what is so remarkable about them. Symbols have an angelic, "prevenient-grace" quality about them: like messengers from on high, they come to our assistance even before we realize we need help. They anticipate our most basic needs and almost always "catch" us by surprise, with little or no advance warning of either their coming or their going. Thus any reluctance or failure on the part of the celebrant to enlist the religious imagination of the faithful in the liturgical rite renders the Christian symbols powerless. What we end up with are invitations that do not beckon, stories that do not surprise and symbols that no longer mobilize or transform.

Language and Communication

There is another important area where the Church lacks imagination, namely, in its official communications, speech modes and use of words. The crux of the problem is a question of communication. In this situation, we are no longer dealing with religious symbols as such (although even words are symbolic), but, rather, with linguistic signs, the use of words and how they are received, if meaningfully at all, by the faithful. A lack of imagination in this area is especially troublesome for an increasing number of Catholics today, with far-reaching consequences for the way they hold and live their faith in today's world.

The problem can be stated thus: *The official inherited language of the Church, venerable as it is, no longer corresponds to the religious sensibilities of a growing number of Catholics, nor does it resonate with their everyday lived experience.* There is a dysfunctional break between the faithful's experience of life in today's world and the official religious terminology and liturgy through which they are expected to "faithfully" express or pray that faith. They fail to experience a real and meaningful connection between the sacraments they celebrate, the hymns they sing and the readings they listen to, on the one hand, and their everyday lived experience in the market place, on the other. Meanings are found not only in words but also in people, and the meanings of the words depend on the people, that is, on the experience of the user and the receptor. Another important principle in communicating well is that the meaning of words and expressions comes from the interaction between information and context. Neither of these two principles seems to be taken into account in the way the Church communicates. As well, the more the needs of the receptor are taken seriously, the more effective communication is likely to be. Canadian sociologist Reginald Bibby, describing these dysfunctions in his book *Unknown Gods,* says that the churches have a fourfold problem: first, a structural problem in that they still rely heavily on volunteers at a time when people's lives are busier than ever; second, a hesitancy to get in touch with and meet the real needs and wants of the faithful; third, a slowness to reflect the social changes that people are experiencing today and a reluctance to take these changes into account when proclaiming the gospel message for our times; and fourth, a difficulty in giving a sense of outreach and mission to their flock, rather than merely a personal piety and devotion.

In this ecclesial context, therefore, the present crisis in language and the communication of faith is not to be interpreted as a general loss of faith, as some are quick to suggest. It is not so much that Christian faith is collapsing in today's world, but that much of the Church's religious vocabulary, in which the faith has been cast and transmitted in ages past, has now become "out of reach" for and "out of touch" with the average lay person today. Nor is the challenge merely one of re-educating the faithful in the Church's traditional speech modes, although this, too, is important. What is at stake is a clash between two very different "linguistic paradigms." Why is it, for example, that church officials still insist (and insist they do!) on using linguistic sexism in official liturgical texts and documents? There is an obvious bias in our modern languages towards the masculine gender, while at the same time, a heightened sensitivity about this bias which is not reflected in the Church. Why is there such a disparity between the Church's official way of expressing and proclaiming the faith and the actual lived experience and sensibilities of the faithful? Since our image of God defines and orients our whole way of life and sustains our moral universe, the exclusive masculinity presumed in the traditional doctrine of God has profound consequences for the way we envisage (and legitimize!) the institutional structures of the Church and its clergy. With a little more religious imagination, is it not possible to remain faithful to a living tradition while not necessarily using the same archaic religious expressions and vocabulary?

What compounds the problem even further is the fact that many Catholics are seeking and finding religious experience outside the visible boundaries of the institutional Church, and they cannot adequately express or communicate this experience in the time-honoured religious vocabulary they have inherited. Religious sensibilities have changed to such an extent that much of our inherited religious vocabulary is unable to do justice to the way we "carry" and "live" our faith today. The faithful understand very well that it is futile to try and put "new wine in old wineskins." At the same time, there is a corresponding reluctance on the part of church officials to create and make available to the faithful "new wineskins," new religious speech modes – especially in the Church's liturgical texts – that would make for greater congruence in the religious heart of the faithful. Meanings are found not only in words but also in people, and the meaning of religious words and expressions depends on the people, that is, on the faithful as much as on church officials.

The myth of a "fixed" and unchanging religious terminology flies in the face of historical evidence. Throughout the Church's history and with considerable creativity and imagination on the part of theologians, the language of faith has always evolved and developed. And Christians of every age and generation have always responded differently, yet no less faithfully, to Jesus' question: "But who do you say that I am?" (Mark 8:29). We cannot have access to the Gospel apart from some kind of human formulation. Yet words carry much more than denotative meanings; they are the vehicles of all kinds of emotional and cultural connotations as well. We must realize, too, that human words are never "fixed" in their original meaning once and for all; they take on a dynamic life of their own, and are always subject to an evolution in their meaning and connotations.

Take, for example, the English word "enthusiasm," the way it has evolved over the centuries and what it has now come to mean.

This borrowed Greek word first entered the English language in 1579 and, until 1608, was always written using Greek letters. In its original meaning, it had the sense of being possessed by a god or being divinely inspired. In the first hundred years of its existence in English, the word *enthusiasm,* and its related forms (*enthusiast, enthusiastic*), had negative connotations and was a term of reproach: it designated a person as having a warped or ill-regulated religious emotion. An "enthusiast" was a person poisoned with the notion of being divinely inspired, when, in fact, he or she was not. During the religious turmoil in Britain in the seventeenth and eighteenth centuries, when the Anglican Church saw itself in dire conflict with both the Catholic Church and various Protestant groups, the word "enthusiasm" came to signify unorthodox and seriously misguided religious beliefs or states of mind. It belonged to the same lexical field as the words *bigotry, infidelity* and *credulity.*

However, as the word "enthusiasm" shifted and moved into the domain of literature and politics, it acquired positive connotations, related to creativity, literary genius and political eagerness and fervour. The *Oxford English Dictionary* gives the current sense of the word as "an intensity of feeling in favour of a person, principle, or cause; a passionate eagerness in any pursuit." Thus the modern use of the word "enthusiasm" has evolved and completely lost its negative connotations. Today we speak of a football enthusiast, a bird-watching enthusiast, a Formula One racing enthusiast, etc., all denoting a depth of interest and admiration with no touch of negative disapproval.

What is interesting to note is that throughout its 400-year history in the English language, especially in the early nineteenth century, there were many who protested the changes they saw taking place with the word "enthusiasm." They tried to fix the term, not unlike the Roman Curia in the Vatican today that tries to "freeze" religious and theological terminology as though in a time capsule. I have taken care to dwell on the historical evolution of "enthusiasm" simply to illustrate how words and their connotations do change, and that even the words used in the communication and transmission of the faith suffer the same fate as those in the secular domain. They take on a life of their own, are affected by cultural changes and sensibilities, and resist any attempt to arrest or fix their original meaning.

What lies at the heart of the Church's communication problem and the dysfunction that exists between the lived experience of the faithful and their inability to "connect" with much of the Church's religious terminology is the belief, in the thinking of the Roman Curia, that the essential message of Christianity is *supercultural*. Their presumption is that faithfulness to the gospel message means that it can be translated word-for-word into any culture without taking into account the unique structures and patterns of different cultures. It is as though every culture is thought to be basically the same and that the gospel message can be transferred to the receptor-language in all its "naked purity," without in any way being altered or "contaminated" by the receiving culture. A good translation, as any student of foreign languages knows, requires more than this kind of literalist approach. It requires a "listening heart" and a highly creative imagination to capture the spirit of a text. In its literalist understanding of what it means to be faithful to the gospel message, the Roman Curia sees but dimly the real meaning of a truly inculturated Christian faith.

The importance of a precise context for clear meaning is always vital in any communication. The real meaning of words and expressions comes precisely from the interaction between information and context. We see this, for example, in the development of dogma and in the way such terms as *redemption* and *grace* have evolved and taken on an amazing variety of new meanings and connotations. This, too, is a vibrant sign of creative theological imagination. But the exercise of religious imagination in the Church cannot be left solely to the "experts," the liturgists and the theologians. The creative imagination of the laity must also be consulted and allowed to participate in this "breaking" of the Word.

Sacred Art in the Church

Sacred art in the North American Church is another area where religious imagination is found wanting. Although the spoken or written word is the most frequent means of communication, there can be no doubt that the arts are also very important for the health and well-being of the human soul. This is true of all the arts, whether essentially temporal (like music and poetry), spatial (like painting or sculpture) or spatial-temporal (like theatre or film). Unfortunately, there is very little in the typical North American parish church today that would qualify as genuine *sacred* art. What we have in so many of our churches is slick, commercial kitsch. As recently as 1948, John La Farge noted that the quality of Catholic art is very poor:

> The fact that Catholic religious art in this country is as yet very unsatisfactory, to say the least, that it certainly does not correspond either to the content of thought and emotion or even in its technical skill with the dignity and competence that our Faith would demand is so much of a truism that it would only be wearisome to labor the point.[8]

Such a statement remains as valid today as when La Farge penned it half a century ago. For instance, anyone entering a typical Catholic church − even those churches recently renovated by commercial companies and "church goods" manufacturers − is confronted with shallow "decorative" art rather than sacred art. When you have seen one such church with commercially produced statues of Mary or St. Joseph or the Sacred Heart, it is as though you have seen them all! There is no religious depth to them, no aura of mystery about them; in their frozen, stylized form, we could say of them, like the psalmist, "They have mouths, but do not speak; eyes, but do not see" (Psalm 115:5). Nor do they create or evoke zones of transcendence beyond, behind or beneath their exterior plastic shape and veneer finish. What you see is what you get! Regrettably, the Church is no longer the mistress or patron of artists today, as she undoubtedly once was. Instead, dealers and manufacturers have rushed in to fill this near-vacuum and have flooded the market with a vast array of cheap, hastily produced and shallow works which appeal to the lowest level of religious sensibilities − the maudlin. Even the statues produced in Oberammergau, the German town famous for its Passion Play, are nice but lifeless. Today they are made with cutting wheels instead of emerging from the hands of artists. Consequently, they do not produce an encounter with mystery, which flows through the artist's hands and comes out a work of living art. The paintings, statues and liturgical hymns that the faithful are now exposed to are, for the most part, of mediocre quality, tinged with insipid dullness and all too frequently with commercial emptiness and no mystery.

Sacred art in North America has not only become commercialized but it has been trivialized; it has become little more than a superficial, decorative embellishment of the sacred and the holy. I recently attended Mass in a relatively new parish church in Canada and soon found myself terribly distracted. From where I was sitting in the middle of the assembly, I began counting the number of crosses my eyes fell upon. The total number, you ask? No fewer than 96 crosses![9] This is what I call the trivialization of Christianity's defining and most sacred religious symbol. In this parish church, as in so many others, the cross is reduced to little more than a decorative sign and ornament. A religious art that does little or nothing to help people replicate Moses' encounter with the Lord on Mount Horeb ("place of encounter"), that does not allow the faithful to experience the "Holy" as Moses did on that occasion, drawn as he was by the flame of fire burning in the middle of a bush and repelled by its demands, and whose only dubious purpose is that it saves people from having to exercise their own religious imagination, is very far removed from what we could legitimately call sacred art. As Thomas Merton once rightly suggested, bad religious art is even spiritually harmful: "The prevalence of bad so-called sacred art everywhere constitutes a really grave spiritual problem, comparable, for example, to the analogous problem of polluted air in some of our big industrial centers."[10]

There have been individual artists who have made exquisite religious works, but these tend to be found in museums, not in our churches. I think immediately of Jacob Epstein (1880–1959), one of the greatest sculptors in the last century, and his profoundly humble *Visitation*, his powerful *Jacob and the Angel* or his *St. Michael Casting Down Satan,* and also of Georges Rouault (1871–1958), the French Catholic painter, whose works, like the *Face of Christ*, are a passionate revelation of faith, and not simply a recitation of faith. The Mexican-American artist Enrique de la Vega created superb statues of *Our Lady of Guadalupe* and *Jesus and the Children,* and Normand Rondeau made exquisite tabernacles, retables and Easter chandeliers, some of which can be seen in Loretteville and Berthierville, both in Quebec, Canada. William Kurelek (1927–1977), one of Canada's best known and most prolific artists, created religious paintings which challenged Canadians to accept religious faith in a secular society. His series on the Passion of Christ illustrates the Gospel of Matthew from the Last Supper to the Resurrection. Would that every church had a work by Fr. Herman Falke of Ottawa, especially from his "Sculptures of the Passion" series. "In my art," he says, "I want to touch the unconditional realness of his humanness." So there are, even today, artists who manage to produce great works of sacred art, which generally find their homes in secular museums instead of sacred places of worship.

In an address to artists, Pope John Paul II described what he deemed genuine artistic intuition:

> Every genuine artistic intuition goes beyond what the senses perceive and, reaching beneath reality's surface, strives to interpret its hidden mystery. The intuition itself springs from the depths of the human soul, where the desire to give meaning to one's own life is joined by the fleeting vision of beauty and the mysterious unity of things.[11]

Would that this most apt description of artistic inspiration was more in evidence in the art and music of our churches today! The Church used to be known as the "patron" of the arts at one time. Now, at least at the local parish level, the only remaining question is, "Where have all the artists gone?" The world of art and the world of faith have become so estranged, so removed from one another that the Church must strive to forge a *new alliance* with artists. Opinions differ concerning the reasons for this historical rift and estrangement between the Church and major artists. Clearly, there are social, cultural, theological and "political" factors that come into play here. And there can be no doubt that monetary constraints play a large role in the proliferation of mediocre religious art and music in our churches.

Every contemporary pope has spoken about the need for a renewal of the arts in the Church, but it was Pope Paul VI who felt this need most deeply. Paul VI, a man who had a deep appreciation of the spiritual vocation of artists, who was sensitive to what constitutes "sacred" art and who also enjoyed intimate friendships with

artists, put his finger on the real cause of this estrangement between the Church and the great artists of our day. Addressing an
international group of artists gathered in the Sistine Chapel in
1964, in what was then a rare *mea culpa* on the part of the official
Church, he said:

> To be courageously sincere, we recognise that we, also, have frus-
> trated you. In fact, one of the first rules we imposed upon you
> was the rule of imitation – on you who are such dynamic crea-
> tors and in whom a thousand new ideas sparkle about a thou-
> sand new things. We told you: "We have this style, you must
> adapt; we have this tradition, you must remain faithful to it; we
> have these masters, you must follow them; we have these rules,
> you must not depart from them." In so doing, we have at times
> imposed upon you a heavy mantle of lead, as it were; forgive us
> for this! What is more, we also abandoned you. We didn't ex-
> plain ourselves to you; we didn't introduce you into that secret
> chamber where the mysteries of God make the human heart
> leap for joy, for hope, and become intoxicated. We didn't enlist
> you as disciples, friends, or partners in dialogue; that is why you
> didn't recognize us.[12]

The blame cannot be put entirely on the doorstep of the
Church; professional artists, too, have gone their own way, and like
Pope Paul VI says, give little sign or evidence of turning their interest to sacred Christian art. At one time, religious and biblical
subjects provided the main inspiration for artists. Today, few quality art galleries even display religious works, a happy exception
being in Chicago, which boasts more than 2.3 million Catholics
and where one can see at least one permanent gallery dealing in
original Christian art. Just how many Catholics in the archdiocese
frequent this gallery is another question. Thus for lack of exposure
to sacred art in their churches, the faithful are obliged to settle for
the commercial, religious schlock found in most religious-article
stores.

Clearly, there is a question of education involved here. Unless
the faithful are exposed to quality works of sacred art, they will
not demand them of their pastors and bishops. On this score, however, Catholics have unfortunately been led to believe that everything pertaining to the art, music, architectural design and furnish-

ing of their parish church has properly belonged in the hands of the clergy and the bishops. The irony is that this practice has often resulted in "the blind leading the blind." Recognizing their own lack of competence in artistic matters, however, the pastors and bishops have often entrusted this important responsibility to competing commercial companies. Without proper exposure to genuine works of sacred art, there can be no artistic education. Sacred art is one of the best formative instruments for initiating a community into the ineffable beauty and mystery of God.

The underlying problem is not that the faithful lack religious imagination. To the contrary, they have much more imagination than is generally credited to them. The real problem is that throughout the liturgical movement and the many changes that have taken place at the parish level following the Vatican Council, the faithful were never seriously consulted nor was their faithful imagination ever appealed to as a guiding "kindly light." Instead, an overly didactic explanation was given to them about what was happening, much to their bewilderment. I can still recall the way the homily at Mass was little more than a teaching moment to explain the changes that were afoot in the Church. Reason and better understanding, not religious imagination, were thought to be the best way to "initiate" the faithful into the new liturgy: if they "understand," everything will be fine! What was overlooked in dealing with an *initiation* process like this (as distinct from a mere learning experience) was that imagination is more important than rational explanation.

In his seven-volume work on theological aesthetics, *The Glory of the Lord*, Hans Urs von Balthasar gives the following warning:

> No longer loved or fostered by religion, beauty is lifted from its face as a mask, and its absence exposes features on that face which threaten to become incomprehensible to man. We no longer dare to believe in beauty and we make of it a mere appearance in order the easily to dispose of it.... Our situation today shows that beauty demands for itself at least as much courage and decision as do truth and goodness and she will not allow herself to be separated or banned from her two sisters without taking them along with herself in a mysterious act of vengeance. *We can be sure that whoever sneers at her* [beauty's] *name*

as if she were an ornament of the bourgeois past, can no longer pray and soon will no longer be able to love.[13]

What all this, in fact, means is that in the aftermath of Vatican II and the many changes it brought about, *pedagogy* took precedence over *mystagogy*. While both are necessary, the difference between the two can hardly be exaggerated. When one is confronted with a problem, one is instructed. But when one comes into the presence of mystery, one needs to be initiated. The language and approach of a pedagogue, moreover, will generally be more conceptual, rational and logical. The language of the mystagogue, on the other hand, like that of the poet, the artist and the saint, is essentially a language of mystery and imagination, one that invites us to transcend and "cross over" to a deeper level of reality, a level beyond what can be adequately expressed in human terms or categories. It is to this crucial difference between pedagogy and mystagogy, and to the crucial role of imagination in the latter, that we now turn our attention.

Part II

Who Is Lazarus?

A member of the family of Bethany,
and brother of Martha and Mary,
Lazarus was an object of deep affection
not only to his sisters, but to Jesus,
which speaks well of his character.
John D. Davis

3

The "Way" of Imagination

We sin against the imagination whenever
we ask an image for its meaning, requiring
that images be translated into concepts.
— James Hillman

To the question "When you think of God, what do you see?"
Christians of every age and every culture have come up with
some mental image that is at once steeped in the living tradition of
the Church, their culture and their everyday lived experience. The
way our religious imagination helps us to relate to, and stand before, a transcendent God will be the focus of this chapter. We will
attempt to follow the Christian imagination as it invites us to put
a certain "face" on God and then as it beckons us to go beyond
any image we may have of him. In short, we hope to show why
our imagination, even more than our reasoning skills, is a privileged and indispensable instrument for any "close encounter" with
God.

Theologians have been somewhat slow to recognize imagination as a vital component in the structure of Christian belief, and until quite recently, they have virtually ignored the play of imagination in their own theological constructions. They seem to have forgotten St. Thomas Aquinas' wise advice that "theology ought to be expressed in a manner that is metaphorical, that is, symbolic or parabolic."[14] This advice comes as no surprise since the West, for the greater part of its intellectual history, has given pride of place to reason, not imagination. Western philosophers, in particular, have not only neglected to deal with the concept of imagination, but have dismissed what they considered an essentially irrational faculty. Convinced that imagination had little or nothing to do with the pursuit of truth they, by and large, relegated imagination to the "fanciful" realm of poetry, art and literature. Despite this Western bias, however, imagination could not be so easily ignored or dismissed; it plays too pervasive a role in so many areas of human life – including the life of faith – that sooner or later its presence had to be reckoned with. When we see just how the imagination functions and the path along which it beckons us to journey, we will come to appreciate it as a guiding "kindly light" rather than an unruly *"enfant terrible."*

Before tracing the sequential stages through which the imagination will take us, two preliminary remarks are in order. The first thing to note about imagination is its *invitational* character: it neither forces nor demands that we follow it to where it would ultimately lead us. Compared to imaginative thinking, which only invites and entices, rational thinking is very aggressive. Rational thinking seeks to "seize" and "get a hold" on reality. In fact, both "apprehension" and "comprehension" derive from the Latin *praehendo,* which means to " grasp," "seize" or "arrest." Imagination, on the other hand, only "invites," "beckons" and "entices." It merely sends out an invitation, as it were, which we can either accept or turn down. It does not impose a logic on us. It is this very capacity to lure, entice and seduce that gives it a special affinity with the way God deals with us, as when the prophet Jeremiah says, "You have seduced me, O Lord, and I have let myself be seduced" (Jeremiah 20:7; Jerusalem Bible). This seductive quality is precisely what makes imagination so congenial to transcendence. It respects our human freedom and never compels us through any power of logic or clear evidence. At any given moment, we can "turn it off," so to speak, and refuse to be entertained by our imagination. We can refuse to be seduced by its inner promptings and can revert back to our customary rational way of thinking. Furthermore, we can do this without feeling guilty or incurring the slightest adverse social stigma. This is more than can be said for those occasions when, in a moment of folly, we decide to throw reason and logic to the wind.

A second thing to bear in mind about the imagination, apart from its deep affinity with the way God seduces us while leaving our human freedom intact, is that, like Lazarus of Bethany, it too belongs to a family. The imagination has "sister" faculties that are at a loss without it – as Mary and Martha were at a loss without Lazarus – and it co-operates very closely with all these sibling faculties. We are prone to make clear-cut distinctions between the human faculties of reason, will, memory, imagination, etc., as though each one of them functions pretty much independently of the others. Such a mechanistic model of the human soul, which can perhaps be traced back to Plato, views the human mind as though it were composed of quite separate interacting parts – indeed, not unlike the carburetor, cylinders, battery, fuel pump, etc., in an internal combustion engine. While we are inclined to assign a special function to each individual faculty, we must not lose sight of the fact that they co-penetrate and depend on one another far more than is generally recognized. Indeed, it can be said that they function as one. In order to safeguard this fundamental unity, we should perhaps use adverbs instead of nouns when referring to them. Thus we can speak of a person who thinks logically and rationally, thinks imaginatively or intuitively, thinks wilfully, poetically or affectively, etc. Although arrived at from a slightly different perspective, my views here are very similar to those of Howard Gardner, the well-known American psychologist and educator at Harvard University. In his influential book *Frames of Mind: The Theory of Multiple Intelligence* (1982), and his more recent *Multiple Intelligences: The Theory in Practice* (1993), Gardner explores the multi-faceted nature of human intelligence and posits several distinct types of intelligence. I concur with his theory, but would add that human imagination comes directly into play in each of these various ways of "knowing," something that is not immediately apparent or explicated in Gardner's work.

That said, let us now proceed to look at the "way" of imaginative thinking and the typical path along which the imagination beckons us to follow.

The Image-generating Phase

It has become commonplace to think of imagination as a creative image-making faculty, for that is what it first sets out to do. This could be called the visualizing stage in which the imagination initially conjures up visual images, sets them before us – both in our waking or sleeping hours – and fascinates us through the sheer vividness of their unusual shapes or forms. When we "see" an imaginary image, say a strange animal or a beautiful castle, we are first of all "struck" and "captivated" by the intense vividness of the image. It is almost as if we were actually present to this object. Some visual form captures our attention and seems to invite us to tarry for awhile longer. In this first phase of the imaginative process, we are presented with some image or representation. What prompts us to actually "entertain" this image in our inner mind's eye is, initially, the *vividness* of the image, especially in one or other of its smallest details or outlines. Something "catches our eye" and momentarily holds our attention. This is why, in this initial stage at least, the imagined object always seems so close to us, almost as though we could just put our hand out and "touch" it! So "real" does the image appear – and yet so strange! – that we naturally tend to dwell on it, however briefly. This is part of the imagination's seductive quality: it flashes a vivid image before us just long enough to surprise us, capture our attention and fascinate us.

In this first phase of imagining, moreover, our "seeing" is not the same as when we are looking at an actual photograph or picture. With the visionary imagination, we experience a sense of inner amazement, a strange sense of familiarity and unfamiliarity, a feeling of having already experienced something quite similar, and yet a simultaneous feeling that we are beholding something altogether new. It is this intriguing sensation of *déjà vu* and *jamais vu* that initially fascinates and holds us momentarily spellbound. In this first phase, the image keeps us guessing at nothing; it just lets us be taken by surprise, asking only that we picture it and hold it. At this point, we can either divert our attention from these musings and re-enter the "objective" world of sensory perception, or we may choose to tarry a bit longer with the image. The great poets, artists and mystics, of course, chose to dwell on their imaginings, expecting and half hoping for "something more" – indeed dimly sensing a mysterious "presence" behind these seemingly strange, unsolicited visitations.

And so we have begun our journey in imaginative thinking, but *only* begun. Already, with its alluring power of enchantment, the imagination beckons us to move on to yet a second stage in our journey and that we shall! But before we do, we must stop for a moment to make some additional observations about this first stage.

Visibility and faith have always gone hand in hand. This is why the Incarnation, God-made-flesh, is such a central mystery in Christianity. Notwithstanding Jesus' remark to the apostle Thomas, "Blessed are they who believe and who have not seen," the Church has always pinned its faith and its hope on the testimony of those first disciples who had, in fact, "seen with our eyes" (1 John 1:1). This close correlation between visibility and faith may also help to explain why the presence of the Holy Spirit in our lives and our world, though very real, is so readily overlooked or forgotten. As Jesus tells us, the Holy Spirit is like the wind: he or she cannot be "seen!" Christians are, on the whole, a visual people, which is why popular devotion clings to its favourite holy image of the Sacred Heart, Our Lady of Lourdes or Guadalupe, the Shroud of Turin and other holy images attributed by legend to direct divine intervention. It is here, at this initial image-generating stage of the religious imagination, that the faithful have always felt most comfortable. The only real danger with popular piety is that it tends to arrest and fix the Christian imagination at this first visual stage. It does not readily seek to go beyond, or to venture any farther, whereas the imagination beckons us, once we have reached this first stage, to move into a second, deeper stage of transcendence.

The age-old controversy about images of Christ and the saints is, of course, well known. The early Christians, influenced in part, no doubt, by the Mosaic proscription to represent the invisible and ineffable God by means of "a carved or molten idol" (Deuteronomy 27:15; New American Bible), were wary of religious images. Yet between the third and sixth centuries, the ancient gods, goddesses and heroes, who had populated the imagination of humankind for a millennium, were gradually replaced by a new imagery of Christ and his saints. The widespread use of religious images and objects by the faithful eventually led church officials and theologians to find some theological ground for legitimizing the use of religious images. They found it in the mystery of the Incarnation, the Word made flesh: Jesus Christ, the Son and icon of the invisible God, who became the central principle for legitimizing representations of "God who is mystery." From then on, the innate propensity of the Christian imagination to generate images was free – free at last! – and would never again be stifled or intimidated; it would go on creating an unprecedented "flowering of beauty" down through the Middle Ages and the Renaissance, which still leaves one breathless today.

What is also of particular interest in this first stage of imaginative thinking is the way the visionary imagination makes us more conscious of living in a world that is far greater than merely that of our immediate physical environment. The imagination makes us aware, if only dimly at first, that we are not confined to this empirical world that surrounds us on every side. It also keeps us in touch and in solidarity with other worlds – indeed, with those who have gone before us as well as those who will come after us. This is what has been called the "contemporizing" function of the imagination: it makes both the *past* and the *future* present to us in a way that would otherwise not be possible. It fosters communion between the living and the dead, between "this" world and "other" worlds. John Henry Newman, in one of his most vibrant parochial sermons entitled "The Invisible World," speaks to this inherent solidarity between "the world we see and the world we do not see."

Another thing to note about this first stage in imaginative thinking is the close similarity between actual physical sight, on the one hand, and imaginative "seeing," on the other. First, physical vision requires some source of light. We need the sun, the moon, the stars or some artificial source of light to see and find our way around in this world. Similarly, the imaginative vision requires its own source of light, namely, inspiration. Like the light of the sun and the moon, inspiration is not of our own doing or making; it comes to us as a pure, unsolicited gift from elsewhere. In Greek and Roman mythology, such inspiration was said to come from "on high," from the nine muses or goddesses of poetry, music, etc. Second, physical vision requires a moderate distance between the viewer and the object of his or her sight. Otherwise, if we are too close to the tree, we miss the forest. Imaginative vision also requires distance, a step removed from the immediate world of the external senses and the intense glare of reality that makes up our daily round. Such *distancing* is especially important in the spiritual life since one of the first conditions for meditation or contemplation is a certain detachment from our immediate daily preoccupations. If one "cannot see God and live," as Scripture has it, we perhaps can, with some modest distancing, at least catch a veiled glimpse of him. Not too close, lest we are blinded by his glory; not too distant, lest we risk losing him altogether. And third, in optics there is a threefold way of visually perceiving an object: (a) *directly*, as when we behold an object in all its immediacy. Direct vision of God, however, belongs to God alone. With all due respect to my saintly mother (who is now in heaven) and her Baltimore Catechism (which is still around), God remains *Mystery* even to those who enjoy the beatific vision, as Karl Rahner so aptly reminded us; (b) we can perceive an object through *refraction*, as when we see an object after it has passed through a medium, like a rainbow through a prism; and (c) we can perceive in a *reflection*, as in a mirror or an image of something original. In the spiritual world, we see only through refracted or reflected vision, as when St. Paul tells us that through faith, we see dimly as in a mirror. This is our only means of "seeing" God, whether it be his mirrored image in creation ("The heavens are telling the glory of God" Psalm 19:1); in historical events (the "Signs of the Times," Vatican II); in sacred art ("Artists have the signal priestly honour of rendering accessible the ineffable and the transcendent." Pope Paul VI); in the often broken image of the neighbour ("I was hungry and you gave me food." Matthew 25:35); or in the

Church's sacraments ("Do this in remembrance of me." Luke 22:19). If we are to "see" God in any of the above-mentioned places, where God allows himself to be seen and lets "his face shine upon us," then the religious imagination of the faithful – our baptismal imagination – must be enlisted and directly involved.

The More Ethereal Phase

The *Oxford English Dictionary* defines the word "ethereal" as follows: *adj.* 1. light, airy. 2. highly delicate, esp. in appearance. 3. heavenly. This is exactly the way our imagination could be described as it beckons us to move on and into a second phase, or stage, of our enchanting journey.

After initially presenting us with some vivid visual images and forms, our imagination then imperceptibly begins to wean us – good spiritual guide that it is! – away from the stark realism and vividness of the images it first flashed before us to lure us gradually to a more rarefied and ethereal level of perception. One might say that we are now being transported to "higher ground," and hence to a level where we can see better and farther. We now experience broader horizons and grand vistas. In the process, ever so subtly, our imagination now would have us revise our notion of what is "real." And with this invitation comes a new way of imagining ourselves, imagining our world, imagining God's presence. We see this happening, for example, whenever we are on a seashore looking out across the vast expanse of ocean, on a mountain looking down on the landscape below, or from a hot-air balloon taking in the panoramic view of the countryside. Does not everything change? Do we not begin to "see" differently, to speak differently, to imagine differently? Indeed, we suddenly begin to see and appreciate, perhaps for the first time, a beauty that was there all along but that had escaped us.

Why are such grand vistas so breathtaking? What is it about the view of the ocean, a starry sky, a panoramic view, or the vast emptiness of the desert that so mesmerizes us and reduces us to silence? Why on such occasions do we suddenly become more receptive, more contemplative? And why are we suddenly flooded with all sorts of musings, reveries and daydreams? The answer, quite simply, is because our imagination is now given more room and freedom to function. It is no longer hampered by the vividness of distinct forms and sharp images. It is set free, not from the real world in which we live and move and have our being, but free from the immediacy of clearly distinguishable forms and images. A whole new way of perceiving reality now comes into play, and in these airy and more rarefied landscapes, the imagination conjures up images that are more fluid, more vague and less sharp. The images no longer depend on accuracy of detail and realistic reproduction. They now become more elusive, less material, much closer to the kind of spiritual images and symbols that the great saints and mystics have handed down to us from their own lofty mystical experience.

We might compare the ethereal quality of these new images to the elusive "manna" that the Lord sent down to his people when they were in the desert (Exodus 16:9-21). "What is this?" they asked in amazement. "Is it *real* food?" Well, yes and no! It was real in the sense that it could sustain them and keep body and soul together. Yet it was most "unreal," as the Israelites quickly discovered, since they could not save or hoard any of it for the following day. It lacked the solid consistency of ordinary food. Nor did it taste anything like the food at the "fleshpots" of Egypt that the Israelites had grown so familiar with. Similarly, we may ask, "Are the imaginings we now behold *real*, or are they pure *fantasy?* Are they of 'this' world or of an 'other' world?" The answer, of course, is that they belong very much to our real world and to that inner dimension we cannot see with our physical sight or fully grasp with our reason. They belong to the betwixt-and-between zone in our being where matter and spirit commingle, where the earth touches the sky, where heaven and earth meet and, ultimately, where immanence and transcendence embrace.

In the process of entertaining these formless images, a step that already marks a significant degree of transcendence, the sudden release of imagination has us now pondering weightier issues, like our mortality, the small place we occupy in this vast universe, the fragility of our being. And with this kind of reverie comes a sense of deep mystery: we somehow feel "closer" to God, and now the images we form of his "face" become very different from the ones we had previously entertained. Surely that is why the desert has traditionally been a privileged place of purification, and high mountains ideal sites for monasteries, shrines and places of contemplation. In such places, we somehow seem better able to *imagine* God.

But even with these newly acquired and more spiritual images of God, our Christian imagination eventually beckons us to move on to an even greater degree of transcendence. It invites us to become a mystic, that is, one who can see far beyond what meets the eye. The great mystics, having reached this point in their own spiritual quest, now resort to the most *primordial elements* in nature to describe their refracted image and perception of God. I am referring to those rudimentary elements that hark back to the origin of human life on earth, such as *earth, air, fire, water.* It is difficult to imagine anything more ethereal than the air we breathe, more evanescent than a flickering flame or more fluid than running water. It is not possible to contain any of these elements, and in truth, we do not "possess" them; they possess us! And precisely because of our lack of ownership, such elements now become the mystical imagination's choice symbols for God.

It is not surprising that Moses experienced his first real "close encounter" with God "in a flame of fire out of a bush" (Exodus 3:2), or that Elijah encountered God, not in the wind or fire but in a tiny whispering breeze (1 Kings 19:12; New American Bible). Even God's discreet and elusive presence in the Holy Spirit, whose name in Hebrew is *ruah*, is compared to the natural phenomenon of wind and breath. It is impossible to lay hands on the Spirit for we know not "where it comes from or where it goes" (John 3:8). The Christian imagination has always depicted the Spirit of God through the great symbols of water, fire, air and wind. While these primordial elements still pertain to the world of physical nature, they do not carry the weight and distinct features that others do. They evoke, above all, the invasion of a subtle, irresistible, inviting yet unpredictable presence. At this stage in our journey, God is approached more nearly in what is *indefinite*, rather than in what is definite and distinct.

With the reader's indulgence, I should like to illustrate this further by quoting Bernard of Clairvaux's description of his own personal experience of God's elusive yet very real presence. In his commentary *On the Song of Songs,* he says:

> I admit that the Word has also come to me – I speak as a fool –
> and has come many times. But although he has come to me, I
> was never conscious of his coming or his going. And where he
> comes from when he visits my soul, and where he goes, and by
> what means he enters and goes out, I admit that I do not know
> even now.... I have ascended to the highest in me, and look! the
> word is towering above that. In my curiosity I have descended
> to explore my lowest depths, yet I found him even deeper. If I
> looked outside myself, I saw him stretching beyond the furthest
> I could see; and if I looked within, he was yet further within....
> So when the Bridegroom, the Word, came to me, he never made
> known his coming by any signs, not by sight, not by sound, not
> by touch.[15]

It is the religious imagination that enables us to have similar mystical experiences. Such fleeting yet privileged moments are reserved not only for the great saints and the great mystics. Every Christian has similar experiences of transcendence, what Karl Rahner calls "everyday mysticism." We are apt to experience the Nameless Mystery, he contends, when we accept a responsibility in freedom even though there is no apparent offer of success or personal advantage; or again, when we pray into a silent darkness, confident that we are being heard, although no answer seems to come back to us.[16]

Perhaps more accessible than Rahner's complex writing style, but very much along the same lines of thought, is Jeremy Langford's *God Moments.* With examples taken from the work of Augustine, Nietzsche and Bonhoeffer, Langford challenges people who may feel alienated from (or indifferent to) organized religion to examine more closely their life's calling and experience to discover those fleeting and often unrecognized moments when God comes closer to us than we realize. And since God never repeats himself, there will always be something of a "surprise" element in these "God Moments." The great Christian writer C.S. Lewis is a good example. Writing of his personal experience, Lewis was "surprised by joy" one day when he suddenly recognized something truly awesome in nothing more commonplace than a handful of mossy earth from the garden that his brother had handed to him. An atheist throughout his early life, Lewis had experienced prolonged moments of longing since childhood. In his spiritual pilgrimage to Christianity, he perceived that this longing and bittersweet desire, which he suddenly identified as joy, actually pointed to something more permanent and fulfilling, namely, to God. Such singular God Moments of deep insight – what I prefer to call unsolicited moments of grace – are not reserved for great writers or great mystics. Everyone has similar experiences of transcendence. The only difference is that the great mystics paid closer attention to them than we do, and knew how to entertain these *surreal* encounters with God. They had the presentiment that there was something important for them here, and however fleeting these privileged moments were, they found a way of "holding on" to them attentively, caressing them, so to speak, in prolonged periods of reflection and meditation. Every Christian has similar "unrecognized" experiences of God but, unfortunately, has never been told what to make of them. Nor has the Church encouraged the laity to pay closer attention to these privileged moments of grace. By emphasizing pedagogy over mystagogy, doctrinal orthodoxy over religious imagination, the Church does not have a very good "track record" when it comes to fostering everyday mysticism among the laity. This is unfortunate because we still must pay heed to Jesus' words: "Blessed are those who have not seen and yet have come to believe" (John 20:29). The Christian imagination adheres to faith at every stage of its growth and ascent to God. What is at stake here is the crucial difference between what Newman called a *real* assent of faith and a purely *notional* one.

But let us now follow the "way" of the imagination into its third and final phase, where the Christian imagination is now poised to usher us onto the threshold of what the mystics have called the divine Darkness.

The Phase of the "Dark Night"

With the total eclipse of all perceptible images, the Christian imagination now takes us to the nadir and zenith of our journey to God. As someone once said, when it is dark enough you can see the stars! Similarly, the imagination is at its best when it is allowed to function in the dark. Herein lies one of its greatest paradoxes: it is very much "at home" in the night, and functions best when all is still and wrapped in darkness, a point we must now consider more closely.

This is the way St. Gregory of Nyssa sums it up: "At first the revelation of God to Moses is made in light. Then God speaks to him in a cloud. Finally, by climbing up higher, Moses contemplates God in the darkness."[17] St. John of the Cross, of course, calls this last phase the Dark Night of the Soul. Faith exacts and creates this night, which St. John describes as the absence of all natural light. It is of crucial importance for faith to preserve this precious obscurity, to guard it from all figuration and intellectual clarity and to relinquish everything that is sensible and reasonable. In order to dwell and abide in this Dark Night, the soul must yield nothing to ordinary knowledge. It is at this point, according to John of the Cross, that a person passes from an inferior state of meditation to a state of pure contemplation. Real contemplation only begins when all the "lights" are turned off and we are left in total darkness. How is this possible? What allows us to "see" or "imagine" something better in the dark than in full daylight? Why is it that we can "sense" the presence of someone approaching us in the dark more readily than if that person were to cross our path in broad daylight? The answer, I am suggesting, lies in the imagination's uncanny ability to "see" and come "alive" in the dark. It harbours a natural affinity with darkness and those invisible presences we so easily miss during the day.

Night has singular privileges, wrote Leon Bloy, but none more singular than the fact that "God sings in the night."[18] Does this not explain why the Church is keen to keep vigil on the nights before Christmas and Easter? Is this not why contemplative monks have traditionally interrupted their sleep to sing their matins in the dead of the night? And is it not also true that nighttime is still the most propitious time to "make" love, that is, when all the cares of the day seem to be either forgotten or forgiven? Is it not at night, also, while we sleep, that our unconscious self, in connivance with our imagination which never sleeps, is most apt to make us dream dreams we never encountered before? Night is immense and enlarges everything. It strips objects of their precise contours and forms, only to robe them with an eternal quality. Since night is the most faithful image of God, it is not surprising that our Christian imagination likes to withdraw into night's immense domains.

O beata nox! O blessed night! What makes any dark night so special is that if God unobtrusively and discreetly wants to creep into our human history and busy lives (as seems to be God's preference!) he could hardly choose a better time than at night, when we are most vulnerable and have "put down" most of our defence mechanisms. If God likes to sing especially in the night, I suspect it is because the darkness of night transports us unconsciously back to our primordial origins: that deep darkness we all experienced for nine months in the womb of our mother, and prior to that, our even more mysterious pre-existence in the eternal mind and heart of God. Rightly does Leon Bloy call the imagination "the mother of Alpha and the younger sister of Omega."

While recognizing that the imagination plays a role in any ascent to God, some mystics have claimed that it has no place in the "dark night of the soul." They readily concede that imagination is useful for beginners in the spiritual life, especially for meditation, but dismiss it altogether when it comes to the higher stages of contemplation and union with God. The irony here is that despite their insistence on the radically *unimaginable* nature of the divine essence, they are unwittingly obliged to use their imagination even in this Dark Night. The classic work known as *The Cloud of Unknowing* is a case in point. The anonymous author of this work has great misgivings about the imagination, which he sees as our capricious ego gone adrift, if not as the machinations of the devil. He insists throughout his work that it is through "unknowing" that one draws closer to God, that is, through the renunciation of all discursive knowledge and imaginings.

We see the same contradiction in those two great Spanish mystics, John of the Cross and Teresa of Avila. John, in particular, has some very disparaging things to say about the imagination, yet while he, too, concedes that the imagination can and does play a role in the first stages of the contemplative life, he emphatically denies that it has any role in the "dark night of the soul." John insists that God is accessible *only* through love, nothing else. And yet while dismissing the imagination, he then goes on to use it creatively to describe the soul's union with God, comparing it to relations between young lovers, as in the Song of Songs. In fact, John never leaves the royal realm of imagination even while attempting to go beyond it.

Teresa of Avila, too, has some negative things to say about the imagination, yet her own creative imagination is the very basis upon which she constructs her *Interior Castle* and the entire mystical journey through its "seven dwelling places." At the very beginning of her work, she says, "We can consider our soul to be like a castle made entirely out of a diamond or a very clear crystal, in which there are many rooms, just as in heaven there are many dwelling places."[19] It is through her ongoing creative imagination that she is able to take the soul through this "castle" and its "many mansions." The ultimate union of the soul with God takes place in the sixth and seventh "dwelling places," which, as in John of the Cross, are described in the language of betrothal and spiritual marriage. The very notion of "mystical nuptials" is metaphoric and hence the product of a very fruitful and creative imagination. Indeed, this may well be the most apt image one can think of to express the ultimate union with God.

Soon after the death of John of the Cross, this whole question about the imagination's role in contemplation was taken up and studied systematically by many of the first Carmelite theologians and spiritual writers. Some argued against the presence of any imaginary representations in contemplation, while others made a strong case for their necessity. Among the latter, one could cite John of Jesus-Mary (d. 1629), Balthazar of Sainte-Catherine (d. 1673) and Joseph of the Holy Ghost (d. 1736), all of whom were highly respected representatives of the Carmelite School of spirituality. As long as we are pilgrims *in via* here on earth, they argued, contemplation of any kind – whether natural or supernatural, acquired or infused – requires the active involvement and co-operation of the imagination. In their own mystical writings, they show how the play of the imagination, even though unseen and perhaps unrecognized, is nonetheless present. In the end, it was this position that finally prevailed in the Carmelite School.[20]

The one point, however, on which all the great mystics – in and outside the Christian tradition – concur is that God is known in the midst of darkness. There is a sense in which *darkness* has more of God than light has, a "thick darkness" as some describe it. In *The Ascent of Mount Carmel,* John of the Cross tells us that this darkness is, in reality, the light of God, which like the sun, is so excessive that it overwhelms, blinds and deprives us finite human beings of vision. The experience of darkness stands at the heart of Christian spirituality and Thomas Merton, in a memorable passage, highlights this paradox when he says:

> The very obscurity of faith is an argument of its perfection. It is darkness to our minds because it so far transcends their weakness. The more perfect faith is, the darker it becomes. The closer we get to God, the less is our faith diluted with the half-light of created images and concepts.[21]

I know of no contemporary writer who has brought out the paradoxical symbolism and "saving grace" of darkness better than Eulallo R. Baltazar. In his insightful study *The Dark Center: A Process Theology of Blackness,* Baltazar shows how "black" and its correlative terms (night, darkness, shadow, cloud) are used in Scripture not only as negative symbols but also as very positive ones.[22] So it is that God, who is ultimate light, is known by us in profound darkness. We will have to return to this notion of paradox later, a notion which G.K. Chesterton describes as making "the truth stand on its head," since so much of Jesus' teaching does just that: it turns upside-down much of our conventional wisdom and human ways of thinking. The only point to stress here is that it is our religious imagination, not our capacity to rationalize, that can capture and, indeed, savour some of the harsh, paradoxical sayings of Jesus. Without Christian imagination, it is well-nigh impossible to grasp the full truth in much of the "good news" of Jesus' uncompromising sayings, much less celebrate it as though we had found, like the woman in the gospel, something of such great value that we were prepared to do anything in our power to posses it and make it our own.

Such is the "way" of imagination and such is the spiritual journey our religious imagination beckons us to undertake, if we would but heed its gentle prompting and inducements. Let us now turn our attention to the many peculiar "gifts" of the imagination and how the Church, in past centuries, has made generous use of them.

4

Sacred Landscapes
and Imagination

'Tell me the landscape in which you live
and I will tell you who you are.
– Ortega y Gasset

The lineaments of the world we live in are both
seen and shaped in accordance, or by contrast,
with images we hold of other worlds – better
worlds, past worlds, future worlds.
– David Lowenthal

T he two quotations above announce what this chapter is about,
namely, the symbiosis between our imagination and the ground
we walk on and the landscapes that inhabit us. The imagination
has often been vilified because of its perceived "wild" nature, and

its tendency to disregard all rules and laws of predictability. It pays little heed to orders dispatched by our logical reasoning powers and never seems bound to a schedule or a pre-arranged agenda. One could almost say that it lives upon its own substance – or so it seems. The burden of this chapter will be to show how the imagination, for all its will-o'-the-wisp appearance, is indeed solidly grounded in the geography of both our soil and our soul. Imagination is boundless, I am suggesting, because it is bound to the landscapes around and within us. It is to this central paradox, this strange connection between geography and imagination, that we now turn our attention.

Perhaps Clifford Geertz's well-known distinction between a "model of" and a "model for" may help introduce our discussion of the symbiosis between our imagination and the experience of sacred landscapes. It should be remembered that these are but two aspects of a single dynamic, but we may distinguish them if only to better understand what is at stake here. Symbolic imagination as a "model of" pertains to its adequacy in expressing all the dimensions present in a particular experience. Symbolic imagination as a "model for" pertains to its capacity to evoke that experience. In other words, it provides a "watching brief" (Ray Hart) on a certain experience and is the means by which we enter the experience. In real life, our symbolic imagination begins as a "model for," that is, it puts us "in tune" with the social symbol system in which we are born, which initially is not so much our own personal experience as the cultural matrix out of which we experience. It makes us aware of the experiences of those who have gone before us, and it illuminates the depth and density of these experiences. Thus on the one hand, symbolic imagination springs from and *mirrors* the major configurations and landscapes of the culture we live in, and on the other hand, it informs and *shapes* these landscapes. This dual function – the imagination's ability to adequately express our human embeddedness in a cultural setting or landscape and its concomitant ability to shape those landscapes – is what gives imagination its privileged mediating position between mind and body, geographical landscapes and soulful inscapes, objective and subjective reality. As an intermediary, imagination has the primary function of connecting "what is" and "what could be" or, in the words of Heidegger, of integrating earth and sky, the gods and mortals. John O'Donohue puts it only slightly differently: "The imagination," he says, "works on the threshold that runs between light and dark, visible and invisible, quest and question, possibility and fact."[23] This places our imaginative thinking midway between human responsibility and human freedom, between obedience and creativity, between our finite "rootedness" in a particular geographical *place*, and our sense of boundless *space*. It is a mediator between the human and the non-human, between the individual and the world.

This is precisely where the imagination reveals one of its great gifts, namely, the way it takes its origin in the meeting of matter and spirit. In this, it espouses the pattern of the Incarnation and harbours a profound affinity with the mediating role of Jesus Christ. A closer look at Jesus as mediator reveals an uncanny affinity between this role and that of our human imagination. It also helps us understand why imagination has always been – indeed will always be – the "handmaid" of Christian faith and theology. One cannot fail to be struck by the fact that the Jesus of the gospels is very much *of* his time yet *outside* it. Jesus lived in a Palestinian environment and bore its impress. He belonged to a definite historical period, spoke the language of his people, used their imagery and religious ideas, knew and read their Scripture and dressed in the garb of his day. In short, he sprang from the "root of Jesse" and was truly embedded in the history and tradition of his people. The gospel genealogies in Matthew and Luke seek to highlight this, as do his name, "Son of David," and the image in this Advent antiphon: "Let the earth be opened and bud forth the saviour." Yet for all this, Jesus was by no means completely taken in, or imprisoned by, his cultural environment or his religious heritage. To the contrary, those who encountered him felt a basic strangeness in his nature and comportment. They never quite knew how to stand *with* him or *before* him. Time and again they would try to fit him into their ordinary scheme of things – even into their most cherished dreams and aspirations – but they never quite succeeded. Even his close circle of friends and followers was struck by how "strange," "different" and "original" he was. In our Christian belief and understanding, of course, this fundamental strangeness stems from the fact that he was "true God and true man," uniting in his person the divine and the human in an unimaginable and unheard of union.

In Jesus, the incarnate Word, God is both unveiled and veiled, manifested but still hidden, self-declared yet not forced upon us with the kind of clarity and overwhelming evidence that would remove all ambiguity – and with it, the essential *clair-obscur* quality of faith itself. Thus the mystery of Jesus is never given as a clear, incontrovertible fact. Then, as now, Jesus reveals himself only in the shadowy light of human symbols and mediations. In him, incarnation and transcendence are indissolubly conjoined. This explains why Christians regard him as a trustworthy mediator between heaven and earth. He can speak and act in the name of God just as surely as he can speak and act on our behalf. Furthermore, what had hitherto belonged to him by divine right now belongs to us – is truly "ours" in the deep sense of personal ownership. Conversely, everything that is ours in virtue of being human is also henceforth truly his.

So it is with our imagination. Like Jesus of Nazareth, the imagination, too, is very much "in the world but not of the world." It is bound and yet boundless, grounded yet forever going beyond its ground. It, too, enjoys a natural propensity for both incarnation and transcendence, for being rooted and yet uprooting. Unlike our rational human powers, imagination does not approach the mystery of Jesus Christ as a problem or puzzle to be solved. On the contrary, it approaches this (and every!) Christian mystery as initially trustworthy, something with which it enjoys a certain inherent connaturality. Instead of trying to resolve the mystery by comprehending it, imagination is happy to accept and live with mystery. In so doing, it safeguards mystery from any and all overzealous attempts to probe, decipher, seize, appropriate or otherwise completely domesticate it. I said earlier that imagination is the "handmaid" of Christian faith. Perhaps it would be more accurate to think of imagination as the "guardian" and "friend" of faith: a *guardian* because it prevents us from construing mystery as a problem to be solved, and a *friend* because it creates a most congenial predisposition for the reception and nurture of faith. But what is more important for our immediate purpose is to consider the "geographics" of the imagination, how it creates various "landscapes" and how, by entering these, we are given new opportunities for our life of faith.

Geography and Imagination

The word "geography," as I am using it here in reference to imagination, refers to the spatial rather than the temporal dimension of religion. The study of the interaction between religion and geography has become a more central object of critical inquiry, as seen in such recently published titles as *The Shape of Sacred Space,*[24] *Landscapes of the Sacred: Geography and Narrative in American Spirituality,*[25] *Sacred Places and Profane Spaces: Essays in the Geographics of Judaism, Christianity, and Islam.*[26] All these studies recognize the importance of geography in the development of religious sensibility and self-understanding. Why a particular place (Mecca), mountain (Sinai), river (Ganges), city (Jerusalem) or grotto (Lourdes) is considered sacred ground can readily be traced back to some historical event that took place at these sites and the subsequent religious interpretations given to them. The natural geographical environment in which a people or a religious community lives has a significant impact in shaping its religious sensibilities. The city dweller, for example, holds his or her religious beliefs differently than does, say, a person living in the countryside.

This last statement has enormous pastoral implications for a Church that now speaks of a "new evangelization" but has yet to fathom what this really means in practice. It is, one might say, one of those new ecclesial terms that is still looking for pastoral substance and an appropriate theology. It is my contention that if this is to be achieved, the fact that faith and place are symbiotic will have to be taken into account. Symbiotic associations tend to be dynamic affairs, and faith and place are no exception. In microbiology, the term "symbiosis" is intended to bring together all the cases where one or more different species live on or in one another. I am justified in using the term in the present context since faith and place coexist and live on or in each other, thus avoiding the need to determine which one of the symbionts – place *or* faith – is the net beneficiary in any given situation. Faith and geography are symbiotic, and any attempt to articulate a pastoral approach to a "new" evangelization will have to take this symbiosis into account and how the "genius of place" (Alexander Pope) can nurture and enliven our life of faith and vice versa. This allows us to understand better why we need

77

places to think with, and how thinking with them is a sacred communion. When we see from this perspective, we begin to appreciate the importance of the environments we create, on the one hand, and the way we hold our religious beliefs, on the other.

A good example of this interaction between faith and geography is Ronald Bordessa's case study of Finland, which is a predominantly Lutheran country and is also heavily forested. The conjunction of these two seemingly disparate realities is not a random coincidence. As Bordessa sensitively demonstrates, the symbiosis between Luther's doctrine of personal salvation, with its dual emphasis on the "hiddenness" of God (*Deus absconditus*) and on "faith alone," and the characteristic Finnish attachment to the forest as a site for inwardness is very real and runs deep. "Man hides his own things," Luther preached, "in order to conceal them; God hides his own things in order to reveal them." The natural forest, so important to Finns as a physical locus of inspiration and inward peace, thus becomes a privileged venue for encountering the Lutheran *Deus absconditus*:

> The forest is a locus of survival, a place of quiet and seclusion in which the soul can be regenerated. It is a therapeutic environment as well as a shelter in which national culture has been kept alive – a comfortable home ground which no warring adversary has ever been able to conquer. The forest is a symbol of disengagement as much as it has historically been the source of life-giving food and shelter and protection from enemies. By turning inward to themselves and their environmental home, the Finns have cultivated a strong sense of national affinity.[27]

The inwardness evoked by the forest and reinforced by the Lutheran faith is also reflected in Finland's typical architecture, which is notable for its sense of inner expression rather than outward display, its simplicity rather than a flamboyant style. While these and similar studies recognize and document a very real connection between geography and religion, few have explicitly examined the unique mediating role of imagination in this connection and why it is that the imagination is so adept at conjoining the two. Those who have explored the geographical imagination tend to focus their attention on certain topographical features such as rivers, waterways, forests, rock formations and mountains.[28] Not only do all these features play a significant role in our ordinary daily lives but as these studies show, they also fuel and condition our geographical imagination. Others have sought to explore the geographical imagination in the more rarefied area of apocalyptic visions. As one of these studies observes, "the themes and images of mystical and apocalyptic writings are almost always rooted in recognizable geographical realities."[29]

Another area of study where the play of imagination and geography has been extensively examined is in utopian literature. Most utopias fall somewhere between the Garden of Eden of Genesis and the New Jerusalem of Revelation. The one, of course, is a lush, primordial garden and the other is a planned, geometric, gem-studded city; the one harks back to our primeval roots and origin, while the other looks ahead toward our dreamed-of ultimate destination. In their superb overview of utopian literature, Porter and Lukermann have examined the evolving geographical extent of utopia and the reason why some utopias are more inclined toward Eden while others lean toward the New Jerusalem:

> First, much utopian literature reflects a deep sense of loss. We have been driven from the Garden and long to return. We no longer live harmoniously within nature. Second, much modern utopian writing looks toward the realization of a better world, the creation of a celestial city. In this literature sentiments of nostalgia and loss are replaced by the spirit of progress, the purposeful march toward an ultimate goal.[30]

The vital role of the imagination in its relation to geography is much more dynamic and pervasive than even these otherwise excellent studies would indicate. Keeping in mind the typical "play" of imagination outlined in Chapter 3, and bearing in mind, also, the mediating role of imagination discussed above, let us consider more closely the fundamental reason why imagination and geography are so inextricably bound to one another and why our imagination has a singular power to "sacralize" earthy places and realities.

Geography is never simply the occasional or arbitrary dress of religion; it is the very "grounding" of all religion. The embeddedness of religion in geographical phenomena stems from the fact that geography, like religion, has its origin in the meeting of matter and spirit, that is, the place where heaven and earth join, literally and metaphorically. What we call "geography" – the earth's physical features, resources, climate, etc. – is both earthy and spiritual. It is not merely a dumb, physical object-mass that surrounds us on all sides, but a breathing, life-giving, interactive spirit-subject that carries both a message and a mystery. Properly understood, all geographical realities are kindred spirits that spring from a single and indivisible source: incarnated spirit, or if you will, embodied soul. Every landscape is laced with mystery. This explains why any geographical landscape is capable of "touching" us so deeply. It may be a snow-covered countryside, for instance, a small, secluded valley or path through the woods, a deserted city street on a rainy night or a boisterous school playground where children are let loose. There is no mystification here. As human beings, we simply impress ourselves and our existence upon the landscapes we behold and they, in turn, speak back to us, often taking us by surprise when they do. When this happens, we sense that what is suddenly being conveyed to us tells us something important about the landscape itself, and yet at the same time, we dimly sense that the message is somehow already encoded in the deepest recesses of our souls. Once again, this is where the mediating role of the imagination comes powerfully into play and awakens us to the inherent kinship we have with the world around us. The revelation of this deep spiritual communion is captured and expressed well by poets, mystics and anyone who has not excluded imagination from their lives or their souls.

Today we have a better appreciation of this spiritual communion thanks to the First Nations in Canada and the United States. From time immemorial, Native Americans have always regarded the natural environment as a sacred union between humans and the rest of the Earth community, including the soil, animals, leaves, rocks and the rest of creation. With their eco-spiritual sensibility, Native Americans enjoy an intimate relationship with nature, and perceive their geographical environment as a sensate, conscious entity suffused with spiritual powers, a land-based, life-giving energy system that constantly refers them to the supreme Spirit who inhabits and enlivens everything. They have for the Earth – and the things of the Earth – what Yi-Fu Tuan has aptly called "geopiety,"

that is, a keen sense of their rootedness in the land of their ancestors and a feeling of respect and reverence for it. One of the best
indicators of this geopiety can be seen in the ceremonies that have
been handed down to them through oral tradition and the teachings of the elders for countless generations. These ceremonies become a symbolic way of "naming" the land as well as the ancestors
who still, literally, live and dwell *in* the land. This understanding is
why they approach nature and all things natural with silence, at-
tentiveness, patience, respect and a sense of timelessness. The same
geopiety exists among the Australian aborigines. This is how
Strehlow, who knew them through his field work as an anthropologist and as one who was raised among them, describes their
deep attachment to their ancestral territory:

> Mountains and creeks and springs and waterholes are, to him,
> not merely interesting and beautiful scenic features in which his
> eyes may take a passing delight; they are the handiwork of an-
> cestors from whom he himself has descended. He sees recorded
> in the surrounding landscape the ancient story of the lives and
> deeds of the immortal beings he reveres; beings, who for a brief
> space may take on human shape once more; beings, many of
> whom he has known in his own experience as his fathers and
> grandfathers and brothers, and as his own mothers and sisters.
> The whole countryside is his living, age-old family tree.[31]

We are beginning to see a slow, arduous return of this ancient
wisdom and geopiety in the emerging ecological awareness in the
Western world. We are becoming aware of the need to treat Mother
Earth with greater reverence and our place in it with greater hu-
mility. The new alliance that we seek with nature, however, will
only come about when we can enlarge our horizons by granting
our geographical imagination its rightful and irreplaceable role in
reconnecting what has hitherto been divorced. For it is our imagination, above all, that discloses those unsuspected connections, alliances and solidarities between things that for too long we have
thought unrelated or autonomous. Without imagination and symbolic awareness, it is difficult to see how this millennium will inaugurate a new era of integration in which all aspects of the human and cosmic world are seen as profoundly interconnected and
all creatures, from the least to the most complex, as forming a

living, organic whole. In this regard, the very expressions "Mother Earth" and "human geography" are both indicative of this deeper communion.

The sacredness of the earth is perhaps best epitomized for us in the way we regard cemeteries and graveyards as sacred ground. Let us take a closer look at this. A cemetery is a piece of land made sacred by death. In fact, a cemetery is paradigmatic of all the ground we walk on, but *this* ground, in particular, the cemetery, has remained a sacred place even in our secular world. Why is this? Why have cemeteries resisted the process of de-sacralization? It is because this ground, this *humus,* represents our "resting" place in the deepest, most ontological sense of the word. As sacred ground, the cemetery reminds us of our human roots and oneness with the earth and soil; it reminds us that our essential grounding in the earth is what creates our grounding in reality, our "home," that vital portion of space which we fill with our presence – whether dead or alive! And lest we forget, the Church's annual ritual on Ash Wednesday brings this truth home to us with a very simple yet telling symbolic rite. For us humans (together with every other creature or thing), our insertion into a geographical place is a coefficient of being. Situated as I am in *this* particular space, localization thus becomes an irreplaceable index of my reality and my identity. This is the "place" (the *only* place) where I can be found, where I can possess my soul or lose it. My whole destiny is somehow mysteriously tied to the very place where I find myself and my neighbour at any given time. This explains why we experience such mixed feelings whenever we visit cemeteries – they are *beliefs* about the earth (not just descriptions of it) and beliefs about ourselves as much as the earth.

Cemeteries are ambiguous places and because of this, it should come as no surprise that our imagination "comes alive" when we visit a cemetery. This is because here, of all places, we experience the coexistence of *presence* and *absence* – something our imagination can cope with exceedingly well. There are places in this world that are neither here nor there, neither up nor down, neither real nor unreal. Such places are called "thresholds," those in-between places that mark crucial points of transition, or boundaries, in our lives. Of all such liminal narrows, the cemetery is surely one of the most powerful because it is where we learn things about ourselves that can't be discovered anywhere else. And the imagination, as pointed out earlier, thrives on paradox; it sees a "surplus of meaning" even in those places or events that appear contradictory. In this case, our geo-religious imagination allows us to "see" beyond what actually meets the eye. The departed, who have gone before us and who are entrusted to the earth that once nourished them, are now imagined as both absent and still somehow present to us, "far" and yet "near." Cemeteries not only tell us something about the departed, but the "plot" of ground where they are interred – "earthed" – also speaks volumes about us, "the living." The dead can and do speak to the living, and they do so especially from their last resting place. It makes sense, then, that if you want to get in touch with someone's spirit, you go to where they have been laid to rest.

Cemeteries are ambiguous because they are liminal sites; they constitute a boundary or frontier where many distinct realms meet and commingle. A cemetery belongs first of all to this world. It is "above" ground and yet "below" ground. It is a place of solace and comfort intended primarily for the bereaved. Second, it is a "betwixt-and-between" realm, a vestibule or "holding" environment for the departed, a place between the "here" and the "hereafter." For the Christian believer, life is changed, not taken away; yet in a very real sense, life has indeed been "taken away." And third, cemeteries are also an expression of reverence for the body, not simply as the former vessel or temple that once enshrined the human soul, but for the body in and of itself since it was *this* body that forged the individual's unique, personal singularity – in this life as well as for the hereafter.

While geography locates us in the world – in life as in death – it does not imprison or confine us. To the contrary, it is forever enticing us to travel about and discover new horizons and gain new perspectives. If our imagination is quickened at the sight of a cemetery, it also marvellously comes alive whenever we "take to the road" and journey somewhere. Imagination, we said, is bound yet boundless. This is why any path, road or highway also becomes fertile "ground" for the imagination. It symbolizes an immense feeling of freedom and being emancipated, of being embedded in the earth but not irremediably confined to any one place or limited horizon. Hence in every culture the deep symbolism of journey, travel, pilgrimage or visit is important. Nowhere is this more evident than in the founding American myth of the "Far West," which can still be seen in the restless mobility of most Americans today and their "itch" to travel and the frequent number of times the average American changes his/her place of residence and address. Nor is it by sheer chance that the automobile assembly line was first invented in the United States: Americans have a real love affair with roads.

The same can be said of Canada's "steel myth" which, in 1881, came with the arduous project of building a transcontinental railroad that would extend from the Atlantic to the Pacific. According to Pierre Berton, it was Sir John A. Macdonald's intention "to defy nature and fashion a nation in the process. His tool, to this end, would be the Canadian Pacific Railway. It would be a rare example of a nation created through the construction of a railway."[32] Completed in 1885, the Canadian Pacific Railway joined the romance of technology and the epic theme of founding a nation in the Canadian psyche, and this was to produce one of Canada's more enduring national myths. The construction of this railroad thus moved from being a fact of life to being an imaginative symbol in Canadian culture. The train, the steel railway, has not only marked Canadian life politically, economically and culturally but the railroad has also become a recurring symbol in Canadian art and literature – as celebrated in E.J. Pratt's poem "Towards the Last Spike."

Roads of whatever kind, like cemeteries, are full of paradox. My former professor of philosophy Edmond Barbotin explains it this way:

> The paradox and deep mystery of the road is that it is found both at the point of departure and at the point of arrival. It is the same road which I "take" here *and* which awaits me there at the end. Through one of the extremities it is here, where I am; through the other, it is where I am not but wish to go, even if it be the other side of the world. The road unites the known *and* the unknown, the possessed *and* the hoped for, the present instant *and* the most improbable future, what is nearest *and* what is

farthest off. The road acknowledges, measures, and does away with distance; it accepts it in order to swallow it up; it is movement, life, and mediation.[33]

No wonder the Exodus story became paradigmatic in the Judeo-Christian tradition. No wonder that even before the Acts of the Apostles was written, "the Way" had become a technical term for the belief and practices of the early Church.[34] And no wonder the very idea of "pilgrimage" is so firmly embedded in every culture and religion. There are, of course, many different reasons why people set out on a pilgrimage. Some are looking for inspiration; some desire a new outlook on life, a change of mind and heart, a conversion; some are questioning their life's purpose; some are doing penance; some want to get closer to God; others want to thank him for some favour received. Yet in every age and culture, setting out on a pilgrimage has always constituted a "restorative rupture": The pilgrim interrupts his/her daily routine, leaves behind home, possessions, family and friends, for some distant shrine or sacred site. And since the pilgrim must travel light, this has always signified a corresponding inner disposition of unattached availability before God.

In ancient Israel, the purpose of the pilgrimage was to commemorate some past event in which the Lord had dramatically intervened in that people's history, and as they recalled these events, their hope and prayer was that he would renew such favours on their behalf again. For the Muslim, the obligatory pilgrimage to Mecca is regarded as a unique contact with the divine, the sacred, and for those who undertake this pilgrimage, it is the high point of their religious life. Meaning "visit to the revered place," the pilgrimage to Mecca – the *hajj* – commemorates the divine rituals observed by the Patriarch Abraham and his son Ishmael, who were the first pilgrims to the house of Allah on earth, the sacred Ka'ba. In India, we find the oldest continually operating pilgrimage tradition in the entire world. The practice of pilgrimage in India is so deeply embedded in the cultural psyche, and the number of pilgrim sites and shrines so large, that the entire subcontinent could well be regarded, with little exaggeration, as one big sacred space. There, the primary intention of the pilgrimage is to receive or gain spiritual communion with the deity who is believed to actually be manifest in the image, statue or icon of the temple. To receive the *darshan* of a deity is to have a sight and/or experience of that deity.

For the present-day Christian, setting out on a pilgrimage is neither obligatory nor necessary, but the pilgrim generally makes it for devotional reasons as an act of personal piety, voluntarily undertaken. Yet there was a time, in the sixth century, when pilgrimages were imposed on penitents, when the whole notion of penance was transformed by the Irish missionaries. The crusades of the eleventh, twelfth and thirteenth centuries gave new meaning to the pilgrimage and transformed it into a ritual. The crusaders regarded themselves as pilgrims, and in the eyes of their contemporaries, they were. The vow of pilgrimage was considered sacred, and church law prescribed that no one could break a vow of pilgrimage and be saved. This law applied to the peaceful pilgrim as well as the armed crusader. In some circumstances, a pilgrim might even be bound by the vow of pilgrimage that another had made. There can be little doubt that the issue of granting indulgences also helps to explain the extraordinary appeal of pilgrimage in the Middle Ages, especially towards the end of the thirteenth century, when the papacy began to issue indulgences more generously.

Although the pilgrim's destination is an actual geographical site with which a deity or saint is physically associated, what gives a pilgrimage its single defining characteristic is the way our geo-religious imagination brings together three distinct yet interrelated levels of identity. A pilgrimage is experienced simultaneously as a *spiritual* journey, a *physical* journey and a *ritual* journey. These three dimensions of reality are combined in a single and continuous landscape. And in this multiform landscape, where the past, the present and the future co-penetrate, the pilgrim can thus see where the earthly and the heavenly are conjoined and experienced as one. Geography is thus elevated and sacralized by the imagination. When the poet Seamus Heaney said that landscape is sacramental, he was merely echoing the words of another scholar, Gaston Bachelard, who said, "The imagination is not, as its etymology suggests, the faculty for forming images of reality; it is the faculty for forming images which go beyond reality, which sings reality. It is a superhuman faculty."[35]

We have thus far been canvassing some of the landscapes that still retain their power to haunt, fascinate or otherwise enchant us, even in today's secular world. Whether these landscapes consist in the personal utopias we secretly construct, the deeper insights into reality we are sometimes given or simply the visions we see when visiting a cemetery or journeying along a road "less taken," the imagination is forever opening these up for us, interpreting them, transforming them, making them "speak," and, ultimately, giving them a transcendent quality — a "surplus of meaning" beyond the actual ground from which they spring. We have noted that such inscapes of the human soul carry some geographical features we dimly recognize or are remotely familiar with. This is what makes them so very real and significant and important to us, even sacred. This brings us to the critical question of the relationship between the sacred and the imagination.

Imagination and the Sacred

In order to understand the vital role the imagination plays in any experience of the sacred, it is important to clear up some fuzzy thinking surrounding the notion of the sacred. What exactly do we mean when we declare or speak of something as being *sacred?* What is sacred to us personally or collectively? In the English-speaking world, one source of confusion has been to speak of the "sacred" and the "holy" as though these two terms were virtually synonymous and simply a matter of incidental personal taste. This is a mistake, for the two terms do not cover the same reality. In the Old Testament, the sacred is never an attribute of God; the God of biblical revelation is not sacred, but holy: "Holy art thou!" He was not the "the Sacred one of Israel" but "the Holy One of Israel." Semantically, we use the adjective "sacred" in two ways. First, a person, object or place of worship is said to be sacred because it has been clearly designated (and is so perceived) as having been set apart and dedicated for a religious purpose or rite of worship. We subsequently come to view and speak of such a person, object or place as somehow being "invested" with a certain divine presence or power. Even those who do not personally view them as so invested nevertheless can identify them as a "sacred" object, place or person, inasmuch as they have been conspicuously set aside for worship. It is important to note that in this sense, no value judgment is implied. A sacred chalice, for example, gains no additional intrinsic value over and above what it originally had before it was "set aside" and consecrated for a religious purpose or meal. Any additional respect or reverence it acquires stems from the recognition that it has been enlisted in the service of religion and therefore of God.

Second, and in a completely different non-religious sense, we designate as sacred anything that harbours an especially important value for us, whether individually or collectively. Thus, for example, we speak of life itself, our children, our family, our country or our culture as being sacred – and they truly are to the extent that we attach great value to them. This is by no means an arbitrary use of the term. To the contrary, it denotes human respect and veneration for something we hold especially precious and dear; we "sacralize" it in the hope that others, too, will respect it as being of precious and timeless value. Used in this non-religious sense, the adjective "sacred" involves three distinct though closely related elements. We experience and call something sacred (a) when we feel that it embodies a special value for us as an ideal, something that gives our life and human existence a particular density of meaning (as distinct from those things we consider of lesser importance); (b) when we invest this value with something of an eternal quality, that is, as being essential and permanent in human life, as distinct from what we know is contingent, relative and forever changing; and (c) when, because of this, we declare this human reality to be inviolable. In other words, we deem sacred any human reality that we feel is of great importance, something we want to see endure amidst so much that is transitory, and therefore something we are prepared to defend against any possible violation, abuse or dishonour. More simply put, the sacred can be defined as *that which legitimizes self-sacrifice and interdicts sacrilege.* Whenever we hear a call to sacrifice or otherwise witness an outcry against some major wrongdoing or abuse, we can be sure that something truly sacred is at stake. We should also note that the correlation of sacred to sacrilege is not confined to the religious domain; we find it in the secular, non-religious affairs of the world as well. We have only to read the daily press or turn on the nightly news to encounter the stark reality of sacrilege. One thinks of the massacre of innocent people, the shootings that take place in schools, the hijacking or downing of commercial airplanes, the child sex trade that continues to flourish in many parts of the world, or the recent September 11, 2001, terrorist attack on the Twin Towers in New York City. We spontaneously and quite correctly call such atrocious acts of behaviour "sacrileges" – and, indeed, we do so in the most profound sense of the word as the profanation of a human right we consider sacred.

Before moving on, let me summarize this brief linguistic analysis of the term "sacred" and certain important implications that follow:

• We can and do distinguish between sacred that is *religious* and sacred that is *non-religious*. Hence even a person who does not believe in God or in any formal religion is capable of naming and experiencing the sacred.

• In either case, whether we use "sacred" in a religious or non-religious sense, it is we humans – and not God – who "sacralize" objects, persons and places. This power to invest something or someone with a sacred quality is a basic, innate capacity inscribed in human nature, and in every culture. It is, in short, a profoundly human prerogative.

• It follows then that the "sacred" is not something that is ontologically different from the "profane" (as Mircea Eliade and others would have us believe). Rather, the sacred is *in* the profane world as an in-depth "reserve of meaning" that gives human existence its density and makes us aware of its transcendent character.

Having clarified some of the semantic confusion surrounding the term "sacred," we can now better appreciate the vital role the imagination plays in every experience of the sacred, whether it be of a religious or non-religious nature. The operative word here is *experience.* What exactly takes place when we experience the sacred? What are we made aware of? The first thing to note is that our habitual way of looking at reality changes. When something sacred impinges upon us, our normal way of looking at things changes.

We experience a certain "irruption" in our routine way of looking at things, a sudden discontinuity of vision or perception, if you will, that often brings with it a sense of dismay, wonder and some foreboding. Even though we may not always be able to rationally explain or justify it, our outlook and perception of reality has been altered, however fleetingly. And it is here, at this crucial juncture, that the imagination comes into play. Since reason alone cannot adequately explain the meaning or nature of this "discontinuity" in our normal perception of reality, our imagination retains these fleeting brushes with mystery and prevents them from being prematurely discarded or deemed irrelevant. Whereas reason is prone to dismiss these as unreal, illusory or fanciful, imagination clings to them, like lichen to a rock, and refuses to let them die or go unnoticed. Whereas reason does its utmost to answer any and every question, it is always the imagination that "raises" the question. Imagination is not in the business of trying to bring answers to reason's questions; it would rather *live* with questions "as if" they, more than the answers we might bring to them, harboured some secret mystery too great for human words or comprehension, as when the poet Rainer Maria Rilke exhorts his young poet friend to *live* his questions: "Learn to live your questions," he says, "as if they were written in a language you do not understand. By simply living the question, you may perhaps one day come to know the answer." Imagination thus goes to a considerable length to insure that these signals of transcendence, however fleeting, these "rumors of angels," as Peter Berger has called them, are never completely silenced, ruled out of court or prematurely foreclosed.

As noted earlier, reason makes a distinction between the real and the unreal. Imagination, on the other hand, distinguishes between the literal and the metaphorical, between the factual and the symbolic. Imagination requires neither the presence nor the absence of a reality. In fact, it operates best "in the dark," that is, when the perceived object is no longer visibly present. In this respect, it was indeed necessary that Jesus should depart from the earthly gaze of his disciples, as when he said, "It is to your advantage that I go away" (John 16:7). There is a close correlation between the departure of Jesus (dead and no longer visibly present) and what this physical departure and absence authorized and made possible for the early Christian community. It opened the hearts of the early Christians to new possibilities, created space for hope to be born in their community, gave the early Church the necessary "permission" to begin organizing itself for the "long haul" here on earth and made the early Christians very creative in bearing witness to Christ's resurrection.

Similarly, when we experience the sacred today, we experience it, as did the early Christians, as a discontinuity, a "creative rupture" which, in turn, gives us permission to go beyond what meets the eye, gives us the audacity to hope and the freedom and courage to transcend the existential "distance" between who we are and what we might become, as well as the historical "distance" between what Jesus actually did in his day and what we today are being called to do. The imaginative act not only enables the past and the future to impinge upon the present but it also allows the sacred to impinge sufficiently upon us to make reconciliation and creativity possible, even in today's world.

5

Other Gifts of the Imagination

Imagination is the essential means, humanly speaking,
by which faith becomes possible.
– Edward Robertson

What is beyond all question is that in the field of religion,
imagination must be accorded an enormous role,
seen as an indispensable agency without which the claims
and teachings of religion could never be communicated at all
– far less arrestingly or memorably expressed.
– Ronald W. Hepburn

In an earlier chapter, I tried to show how imagination – religious or otherwise – prompts, lures, entices and beckons us to follow it along its enchanting "way" – a way that initially captivates us with distinct, vivid images, only to lure us into a more ethereal realm and, ultimately, into a "dark night" where, in all vulnerability, we recover the source of our being. Here I would like to analyze the various gifts of the imagination and how they affect us and play out in our daily life as well as in our life of faith. Because of its somewhat playful nature, many fail to take imagination seriously, in much the same way that we generally do not take the play of children seriously. Yet even in its ludic nature, imagination harbours a deep affinity with God's divine playfulness. Meister Eckhart, the influential fourteenth-century theologian and spiritual writer, says that God is like "a person who clears his throat while hiding and so gives himself away." Anyone who has played hide-and-seek knows how true this is: we all love to hide, but we all eventually want to be discovered. This is especially true of God and little children. We also do well to remember the words that warn us about not being able to enter the kingdom of God unless we become as little children. The burden of this chapter will be to examine the various gifts of the imagination, to explain why they are integral to faith, and to illustrate how the Church, in its life, celebrations and theology, has not hesitated to make generous use of these gifts in the past.

The Gift of Sudden Perception or Intuition

The first and perhaps most precious gift of the imagination is the way it suddenly and often, quite unexpectedly, allows us to see something that others fail to notice or appreciate. We all have experienced these thrilling moments of personal intuition in our daily lives, even though we are not always aware of being inspired or so moved. How often do we notice or perceive something that escapes the person next to us or the ordinary observer? Something "catches" our eye, "strikes" our fancy or suddenly "captures" our interest. It may be something as simple as a configuration in the clouds, a word or expression that "leaps" out at us from the page of a book, a particular contour or colour in a painting, a special feature in a person's face or demeanour – something, in short, that others begin to notice only *after* we have drawn their attention to it. My point here is not that some people have a keener sense of observation than others; my point simply is that whenever we surprise ourselves by recognizing something that others fail to notice, this is a sign of the perceptive nature and play of imagination. Furthermore, we ourselves are generally at a loss to explain *why* our attention is drawn to, and momentarily "arrested" by, this or that particular thing or idea. Psychologists explain this phenomenon as coming from the preconscious, the unconscious or the "shadow" side of our personality. Others, following Marcel Proust, suggest that it comes from the "remembrance of things past." Artists, of course, have traditionally attributed it to the muses, while theologians tell us this could be an inner prompting of the Holy Spirit or, indeed, the Devil.

There is obviously need for discernment here, but certainly not before we acknowledge gratitude for this wonderful God-given gift of perceptive imagination. If God invites us to "come closer" to him, such a divine invitation can only come to us via our religious imagination. We must somehow be able to capture a sign or signal, however small, of the divine intent. If not, then the invitation has never been effectively communicated to us. The perceptiveness of the imagination is our inherent natural openness for and means of receiving all these invitations. St. Thomas always maintained that God's grace builds on nature; it does not try to circumvent nature or make do without it. In his play *Saint Joan,* George Bernard Shaw brings this out in furious simplicity. When brought to trial, Joan of Arc is questioned about the "voices" she claims to have heard and replies, "I hear voices telling me what to do. They come from God." To the countercharge that these are in her imagination, she answers, "Of course, that is how the messages of God come to us." When all is said and done, however, perhaps it does not much matter where these fragments of sudden perception come from; what matters is to realize that in each and every such instance, the imagination is directly involved.

The first characteristic of imagination, then, is *perceptiveness*: the capacity to see "something" in a landscape, in the sky or in a score of music, in the face of another person or in a piece of driftwood, which others pass by. Such perceptiveness is commonplace in scientific investigation and discovery. It is also very much at the heart of artistic creativity. Paul Valéry, the great French literary genius and poet, describes it well:

The poet is awakened in a person at an unexpected event, an outward or inward incident: a tree, a face, a "subject," an emotion, a word. Sometimes it is the will to expression that starts the game, a need to translate what one feels; another time, on the contrary, it is an element of form, the outline of an expression that seeks its origin, seeks a meaning within the space of my mind.... Note this possible duality in ways of getting started: either something wants to express itself, or some means of expression wants to be used. And yet we experience this illumination as our very own, for it fills us with the sudden joy of insight and personal discovery.[36]

Such perceptiveness is also an important aspect of the religious imagination and an essential element in the life of Christian faith. We get a glimpse of it, for example, in the autobiographies of many converts to the faith, from St. Augustine to C.S. Lewis – Augustine when he suddenly perceived something while reading Cicero's *Hortensius,* and Lewis when he was suddenly struck by something in nature, the "Idea of Autumn," as he called it in *Surprised by Joy.* We see it especially in the lives of ordinary Christians who suddenly intuit or "see" Christ in the many faces of the needy, the suffering and the poor. Or, again, when a travelling Good Samaritan suddenly gets the "bright" idea to stop and help the neighbour in distress instead of passing on without noticing; or whenever a person hears another utter the simple words "I'm sorry" or "Thank you" or "I love you" – and has the sudden intuition that this, surely, is what Jesus meant when he said that the kingdom of God, though hidden, is already in our midst; or when a mother loses her ten-year-old child in a senseless accident and suddenly recalls, in her grief, having heard St. Paul say something about "suffering with Christ" (Romans 8:17) and "completing what is lacking in Christ's afflictions" (Colossians 1:24).

It is often when we are preoccupied that these flashes of perception or insight burst in upon us, abruptly and unannounced – like the angelic power that burst in upon Mary at the Annunciation to tell her that she would be with child. Unlike discursive thinking, imaginative thinking is more like a kind of "knowing without knowing why we know." Notice, too, that when we experience such an instance of sudden illumination, it happens *to* us, hence the use of the passive voice to describe it. This experience of being acted upon, of "being struck," is beautifully expressed by Friedrich Nietzsche when he speaks of his own inspiration for writing *Thus Spake Zarathustra*. This is how he describes it: "One hears – one does not seek; one takes – one does not ask who gives; a thought suddenly flashes up like lightning, it comes with necessity, unhesitatingly – I have never had any choice in the matter."[37] Whatever their source, these sudden perceptions come upon us quite spontaneously and independent of our will. In hindsight, we get the distinct impression of having been "visited" by some nameless agent or kindred spirit. And yet, once we have experienced such an insight, we feel that it is "ours" in a very *personal* way, something that truly belongs to us as little else in life "belongs" to us. It is this vibrant, uncanny perceptiveness of the imagination that makes us resonate with certain things more than others, that brings us to a second important characteristic of imaginative thinking.

The Gift of Selection

Imaginative thinking is *selective*. At any given time, it chooses something and leaves something else aside. With all the things that daily confront us, including the mass of media data that assails our senses on a regular basis, the imagination seizes upon some salient "piece" of reality and ignores, or is seemingly indifferent to, the rest. Perhaps this is because, as T. S. Eliot said, we humans can take in only just so much reality at any given time. Or maybe it is because if we tried to give our undivided attention to everything that goes on around us, we would become, if not neurotic, then so distracted and fragmented that we might lose our soul, that is, our sense of direction in life. We would become like a ship without a rudder, or a compass that no longer points in any sure direction. It is our imagination, I am suggesting, that saves us from getting caught in a vortex of total dissipation, by helping us to focus our main interests on certain things, events, people or causes rather than on others.

This helps to explain in part why we become very interested, even grossly absorbed, in some things while being indifferent or oblivious to others. We see this selective play of imagination every day, when a person chooses *this* particular vocation instead of another, or likes *this* particular composer rather than another, or *this* particular sport more than any other, or *this* author.... The imagination is at play behind every free choice we make in life. It gently predisposes and lures us to favour some things over others; it quite literally *charms* us into making the preferential choices we make. Nor does its selective capacity stop here; it refines our choices in life still further. Even though Brahms may be my very favourite composer, my imagination enchants me still further since I find myself liking his symphonies more than his concertos, piano music or songs. The selective enchantment of my imagination continues: of the four symphonies that Brahms composed, my favourite is his Third Symphony. And among its four movements, there is something about the third, the *Poco Allegretto,* that really enchants me. It would seem that the imagination has now completed its alluring mission. Not so! There are many recordings of Brahms' Third Symphony, all of them professional and exquisite, yet my discerning imagination leads me to favour the recording of Karl Bernstein's interpretation with the London Philharmonic Orchestra over all the other superb renditions. I may try to explain the reason for my preference, but that can come only *after* my imagination has cast its enchanting spell over me, that is, *after* it has charmed me into making my selection in the first place.

One example – which holds true in every domain and sphere of life, from the most important to the least significant – comes from the world of sports where it is virtually impossible to take an interest in every event. So we make a choice – be it football, NASCAR events or basketball – and become interested in the ones we like and pass over the others. What we often fail to realize, however, is that it is our imagination, more than anything else, that draws us into making these particular selections.

That choices have to be made is obvious. What is often overlooked is the important role our imagination plays in our preferential options. When we fall in love and choose a marriage partner, for example, our imagination is very much involved in making this important, though mysterious, selection. Why an individual chooses *this* particular spouse instead of another remains a mystery that defies rational explanation. The very notion of *falling* in love bespeaks our vulnerability and lack of rational control. The discovery of this "special" person in our life usually comes as a surprise. The interesting, beautiful, thrilling aspect of falling in love, or being loved, is its character of surprise, of unexpected and sudden discovery. The origin of this discovery stems, in large measure, from the way our imagination has enchanted us over time and has made us "lean" towards making the particular choices we make. And it does this, moreover, while leaving our freedom intact. In a very real sense, it is true to say that falling in love is "playing with possibilities" – something for which our imagination is especially gifted.

The same thing occurs in our life of faith. Among all the Church's teachings and doctrines (and her deposit of faith is very large indeed!) we invariably give more importance to some teachings than others. We have our "favourite" saint or devotion, our "preferred" virtue and gospel story, our own unique, personal way of trying to follow Jesus in today's world. We take to heart and give priority to some of the teachings in the *Catechism of the Catholic Church* and unconsciously deem others to be of secondary importance. Again, our religious imagination plays a defining role in the way our Christian conscience is formed and in the way we espouse a subjective hierarchy of truths among the teachings of the Church.

In theological terms, this is what Karl Rahner has called an "existential hierarchy of truths." This simply means that we all give more weight to some articles of the Creed than others. This is not to say that the other articles of faith have no objective importance; it simply means that as far as our own salvation and holiness are concerned, some beliefs are more important than others. If pressed, we might give the other articles of faith something of a *notional* assent, which does not mean we are "religiously indifferent"; it simply means that we are all "different religiously." What prompts us to *be* different in our adherence to the teachings of Christ and the choices we make in our faith journey is due, by and large, to the selective nature and play of our religious imagination. Gradually, and without any coercion, our religious imagination draws us to certain aspects of our Christian faith rather than to others. With its gentle "seductions," it fashions our preferences and, over an extended period of time, moulds our spiritual profile and sense of Christian identity. Those few religious truths we hold most dear become the "core" of our spiritual life, and might lead to our "taking care of widows and orphans in their distress" (James 1:27), or going to church every Sunday. It is precisely here, in the deep centre of our soul, that an alliance between the Holy Spirit and our religious imagination is forged, and this, in turn, explains why we hold and live our faith the way we do.

The Gift of Making Connections

Another thing the imagination does – and does exceedingly well – is to make connections between things we customarily think of as incongruous or completely unrelated. In this capacity, imagination is our most creative alliance-building faculty. The late Yehudi Menuhin, explaining the musician's imagination at work, describes it this way: "Music creates order out of chaos; for rhythm imposes unanimity upon the divergent, melody imposes continuity upon the disjointed, and harmony imposes compatibility upon the incongruous."[38] The process of creative imaginative thinking consists in discovering some link, connection or intimate liaison (Koestler calls it "bisociation") between things that have not formerly been seen to be connected. Frequently, the imagination does this by tearing something out of one context or field in which we have traditionally classified it in order to insert it into a new context, thus creating a new way of "seeing" reality and things that we had previously deemed distinct and unconnected. Essentially, imagination consists in making "uncommon feats of association," as the poet Robert Frost once described it. The genius of creativity consists in seeing what everybody else sees, and then imagining a connection between them that no one else sees. In short, imagination gives us an eye for things previously overlooked. A classic example in science is the way Newton was able to bring together the discoveries of Kepler and Galileo, which hitherto had appeared unrelated, leading him to suppose that gravity was universal and could act at enormous distances. Another example is the way Einstein extended his theory of relativity to include the effects of gravity by associating two opposing ideas, namely, simultaneously "falling" and "being at rest." Although Einstein was allegedly a mediocre mathematician, he possessed a remarkable imagination. It is said that he thought in signs and images which he combined in a kind of imaginary mental game. On reading Maxwell's theorem explaining light waves, Einstein is reported to have imagined himself riding through space, astride a light wave, looking back, like a child on a merry-go-round, at the wave next to him.

This ability to make uncommon feats of association prevails in the religious world no less than in the arts and sciences. Before "the demise of Lazarus" in the Church that we spoke of earlier, at a time when the ecclesial imagination was much freer to make creative connections, there were many such feats of association. One early example is St. Paul's elaborate metaphor of the "mystical body of Christ" (1 Corinthians 12:12f). He saw a connection between the way the risen Christ is united with his faithful followers on earth and the human body, with all its parts functioning as a whole with Christ as the head, thus forming a living ecclesial *symbiosis* (a word that literally means "together-living"). According to Ricoeur, a metaphor is not simply a figure of speech intended to embellish a text or a fanciful way to add colour to something that is already known. In *The Rule of Metaphor* and other essays, Ricoeur situates the role of imagination in a dynamic hermeneutics. He shows how metaphoric language, as an "impertinent predication," has the uncanny ability to shatter the previous structures of our use of language and the way we have hitherto conceived reality.

Even Jesus demonstrated an uncanny ability to make original connections and striking metaphors, as in the way he seized upon the root metaphor of "kingdom" to describe his earthly mission from God, and further using his parabolic imagination, in the way he illustrated what this meant for his close circle of friends. His discourse on the kingdom of God was not simply a reiteration or a colourful amplification of some known reality. It was nothing short of a mind-jolting revelation of a startlingly new "event" in human history, namely, the unimaginable "in-breaking" of God's love and presence in our midst.

We see another fine example of the Christian imagination's ability to discover hidden "connections" in what scholars call "biblical typology," in which the leap of the imagination makes a hitherto unrecognized correspondence between the two Testaments. By means of typology, the two become a single discourse and drama in which Christ is the protagonist. Typology unites past, present and future – the very thing imagination loves to do. Christ is depicted as the "New Adam" and the "New Moses." Mary is seen as the "New Eve," with events of the past foreshadowing something new.

The peculiarity of typology is precisely that through the parallelism of events, it brings to light the unity of the divine plan. In their manuscript illuminations, sculptures and stained glass windows, medieval artists took great delight in interpreting events of Scripture using this typological method. St. Augustine expressed it well in his celebrated axiom: "In the Old Testament the New lies hid; in the New Testament the meaning of the Old becomes clear." If biblical typology has fallen into disuse today, except perhaps as a historical curiosity, this is largely due to our changed way of interpreting Scripture and also, as noted earlier, to our diminished sense of religious imagination and symbolism.

Systematic theology is nothing more than a human attempt to discover, in faith, a logical connection between seemingly diverse Christian mysteries. Theology is basically an alliance-building exercise and that is why the religious imagination comes into play in every theological construction. Ever since the eleventh century, theology has defined itself as "faith seeking understanding." The problem, of course, is that God's mighty works of love do not always neatly fit into our rational categories, therefore evading our full comprehension. Only in the last few years has the notion of theological imagination emerged as essential for "doing" theology today. What we need is a way of *imaginatively* re-visioning the mystery of God, creation and providence so that a connection can be discovered between these Christian mysteries and what we know and experience to be true today. As our alliance-building faculty par excellence, imaginative thinking always comes into play when we deliberately set out to bring about peace and reconciliation. Indeed, the lack of peace, whether between churches, religions, governments or individuals, is a sure sign that imaginative thinking is lacking. Imagination not only builds bridges, it gives us the courage to cross them as well and thus to embrace what we hitherto believed was unthinkable.

The Gift of Extra-temporal Vision

One of the principal characteristics of imaginative thinking, already alluded to, is the way it allows us – indeed beckons us – to treat the past and the future *as* present. It allows us to transcend the lineal sequence of time, thereby permitting us to go beyond the temporal categories of "past" and "future." Our imagination gives us what I am calling its "extra-temporal" insight, or vision, in which past and future merge and are actualized in the present "here-and-now" of our lives. To borrow Nietzsche's brilliant expression, our imagination gives us the "capacity to think unhistorically." Remembering the past and projecting possibilities for the future are not merely instances of "making believe." The imagination allows us to take a step out of time, so to speak, and to see things simultaneously and from a higher vantage point, what the ancients called seeing *sub specie aeternitatis* – seeing reality as if through the eternal eyes of God.

Let us consider for a moment how imagination relates to past events and history. What is history? We call history a sequence of events, often with some causal association, that we perceive as having cohesion or inner logic. What is often overlooked is that all "histories" are, to a large extent, products of the imagination, that is, the hindsight manner in which we link events together, like so many beads on a string; we call the result "The history of…such a person or country." Imagination is not one of the great products of history; it is history that is one of the great products of imagination. In this sense, it is easy to understand the postmodern rejection of all "meta-narratives," whether they be the grand history of a country or civilization or the grand biblical narrative of "salvation history," so called. I say one can *understand* such a postmodern rejection, but, unfortunately, it rests on an erroneous assumption, namely, the belief that the products of the creative imagination are *unreal,* with no grounding in objective reality. The fact that any "given" history will indeed always have to be "rewritten" is not a sign of its unreality, but a sign that the historical imagination is forever creating new ways of looking at things, discovering new connections between events and sensibilities and hence new ways of synthesizing.

When we recall the past or re-enact some past experience, both our imagination and our memory are engaged and collaborate closely. This explains why from antiquity to the Renaissance, one of the best mnemonic devices to help us remember something was to associate it with some image, feeling or design. Although memory and imagination collaborate closely, their *modus operandi* is different. Whereas memory tries to retain our experiences and acquired knowledge as faithfully as possible, in keeping with the original form in which we actually received them, imagination seeks no such conformity or accuracy. It does not try to merely repeat or replicate the past exactly as it may have taken place; rather, by realigning past events into different configurations and by projecting present-day elements of actuality onto our past, it *re-creates* history and thus brings about new insights about ourselves and those who have lived before us. The imagination "composes" our past with whatever we may be presently experiencing. It does not merely *re-call* the past; it *actualizes* the past *as* present. Actualization here means the process by which a past event is contemporized for a generation removed in time and space from the original event, such as the two thousand years that separate us from the life of the historical Jesus.

It is this gift of the imagination that enables Christians today to envisage, know and experience themselves as true "contemporary disciples" of Jesus Christ. Despite the two thousand years that separate us from the events of the New Testament, present-day believers can imaginatively *interpret* and *actualize* them in a new culture and age. Contemporaneity with Christ, then, does not simply mean committing to memory what happened some two thousand years ago. The "memorializing" in question is a real trans-historical encounter and an actual participation of the past *in* the present.

This is precisely what St. Thomas understands and is getting at when he describes the sacraments of the Church not only as signs that recall the saving deeds of our Lord (in the sense of keeping their memory alive), but as signs that effectively re-enact or actualize these deeds trans-historically in the present. He speaks of a threefold contemporizing function of the sacraments: "A sign," he says, "that is at once *commemorative* of that which has gone before, namely the passion of Christ, *demonstrative* of that which is brought about within us through the passion of Christ, namely grace, and *prognostic*, i.e., a foretelling of future glory."[39] Here again we see the religious imagination at work making theological connections between past and future realities and "actualizing" them in the present.

This actualizing role of the imagination can also be seen in the Christian practice of "imitating" Christ, the *imitatio Christi,* which has a firm basis in the mind and purpose of Jesus himself. Imitating Christ does not consists in an external imitation of the character and actions of Jesus of Nazareth, nor does it consist of a blind replication of his deeds or teachings. It is far more demanding than this on the part of the believer: it means taking the risk of interpreting the words and deeds of Christ in an entirely new context of life and historical circumstances. This requires far more religious imagination on the part of the believer than what we generally understand by a master-pupil relationship. It requires interpreting what Jesus said and did in his times and culture and faithfully "inculturating" it in an entirely different set of cultural and historical settings. In short, the Christian today must take the risk of finding the response that the Spirit of Jesus inspires in us in the light of our new historical situation. This dual task of interpreting what Jesus did, on the one hand, and actualizing it in our day and age, on the other, forms an effective trans-historical arc that we call the *living* tradition of the Church here on earth, a tradition that is living precisely because it is steeped in the religious imagination of the pilgrim people of God.

The second facet of the imagination's trans-historical vision relates to the future. It is Senator Robert F. Kennedy who is remembered for the following saying: "Some people see things that are and wonder, why? I see things that never were and ask, why not?" The ability to see things that never were is an act of creative imagination. Imagination gives us the ability to account for what might be. At any given moment, we represent the future, whether imminent or distant, with the help of prefigurations, symbols, imaginative scenarios, visions and urgent longings, all frequently charged with mixed feelings of fear and hope. It is not possible to foresee without imagination. Far from being arbitrary or unnecessary, foresight is deeply inscribed in the very structure of our being, especially in our basic human needs and desires. Imagination, as a form of desire, characterizes our finite, temporal being. At every turn, it reminds us that we are insufficient unto ourselves, that we need some "other" or "others" to become that self we somehow dimly sense is always "before" us, our *true self.* In this deep longing to become the person we feel destined to be, the desiring imagination holds out possibilities before us. With an eye trained on what is "not yet" or "still lacking" in our life, the desiring imagination envisages possibilities that gradually begin to "grow" on us, possibilities that eventually "take hold." These possibilities, in which the prospect of failure is also present, now become occasions for momentous decisions.

Earlier I referred to the "play" of imagination and how to live and to love is to "play" with possibility. I did so advisedly because of the truth-claim and connection between what it means to play and what it means to imagine and entertain real possibilities. There are two things about play that make it so irresistible, even for adults. First, play or game-playing absorbs those who play; we "lose" ourselves in the play. In fact, the more self-conscious we are when playing, the more the purpose of play is frustrated. This is true whether we are playing chess, baseball or performing on stage. This means that the essence of play is not located in the consciousness of the player but in the very structure of the play itself, with its back-and-forth movement. Genuine play absorbs us in a structured to-and-fro movement and hence shapes our consciousness in the movement. Second, play is an encounter with possibility. It is this feature especially that ultimately makes play so human and so seriously engaged in.

In life, even if we are quite happy where we are and in what we are doing, it would be soul-destroying to think that we had no further possibilities. When this happens, we feel that our life has somehow settled into a "rut" with little or no possible escape. When the dread of living without further possibilities becomes too great, one last possibility may cross our minds, namely, the possibility of "taking" our own life. Paradoxically, suicide is always perceived as a last, desperate act of hope, a *possible* "way out." We humans play if for no other reason than to always keep alive the experience of possibility in our hearts and souls. Humanly speaking, play is a saving ritual: it is our most connatural sacrament of hope. We turn to play because the human spirit is always in need of experiencing possibility. In the game of baseball, for example, at the magic moment when the rim of the bat connects with the baseball, the possibilities of just where that ball will go are staggering. Imagine for a moment the baseball (a round sphere) travelling some 90 miles an hour over home plate and hitting an equally fast-swinging bat (also a round object). The possibilities for what happens *next* are nothing short of mind-boggling! The possible distance it *could* fly, the possible directions it *could* take, the possible arcs in the sky it *could* trace or the unpredictable bounces it *could* take – all these titillating possibilities make baseball the enthralling, all-American game it is. And so it is with all play. But what, you may ask, does all this have to do with Christian faith?

It is my contention that the two central features of play – its ability to absorb us into the structure of its very movement and its being a tantalizing experience with possibility – are two of the more characteristic features of Christian faith. Let us now take a closer look at this dual affinity between playing and believing.

For a Christian, faith is first of all the basic conviction that God has reconciled, once and for all, our estranged world to himself in the person of Jesus the Christ. The gift-quality of his gracious action, as both Creator and Redeemer, initiates and establishes the very structure of faith itself. It sets up a two-way, back-and-forth movement between God and the believer, a divine structured movement into which the believer becomes absorbed to such an extent that, as in play, it shapes his/her consciousness in its movement. In the process, it becomes an outward manifestation or epiphany in the world through the participating believers – a contagious "spectacle" and an object of public attention. The result is Christian witness *in* the world but not entirely *of* the world. *In* the world because that is where we live and move and have our being, where the Christian community becomes a sign that the self-communication of God's infinite love has indeed been communicated, received and is now being acknowledged. Yet not entirely *of* this world because God's gracious action is quite "out of this world!" – literally and figuratively – almost too good to be true, and yet opening up for us some new possibilities. Thus, as in play, the very structure of Christian faith is set up through the reciprocal "back-and-forth" movement of divine gift-giving and human response. A gift becomes a gift only when it is received and recognized as such. It is the enactment of this structure, the to-and-fro movement within faith itself, that absorbs the Christian into it – even to the point of realizing that "they who *lose* their life will save it."

The second aspect of play, as an experience with possibility, is even more evident in the process of believing. Christian faith is the perception of possibility, including the possibility that "miracles" can and do happen. The Christian imagination is quite at home with the gospel episodes of Jesus walking on the water to join his distressed disciples in their storm-tossed boat (Matthew 14:22f) or passing through the closed doors that we ourselves have locked (John 20:19) – in short, that anything is possible with God (Luke 1:37). Nowhere does the Christian "lose" him or herself more sincerely and with a greater sense of possibility than in prayer. When we pray, even when asking God for the impossible, we have entered deeply into the structure and "play" of faith. It is the believer's way of returning the "ball" to God's court, of giving God yet another chance to convince us that he has not made a mistake in creating the likes of us human beings, that he can indeed hear and be inwardly moved by our prayers. And whatever the final outcome of our prayers for the impossible, we want to be able to accept his will. "Faith is the assurance of things hoped for, the conviction of things we cannot see," says the author of Hebrews. It is here that the faithful religious imagination – the grace to believe and, indeed, even to "hope against hope" (Romans 8:18), if need be, that things could be different – comes into play. For the believer, Christian hope places no restrictions and places no bounds. The structure of faith, like play, lies in the discrepancy between what actually is, and what could be. And the greater the discrepancy, the more our faithful imagination is called forth.

Part III

Feeding off the Crumbs

Lazarus came out, tied hand and foot

with burial bands, and his face was wrapped in a cloth.

So Jesus said to them, "Untie him and let him go."

John 11:44

(New American Bible)

6

Holy Terrors: Yesterday and Today

The fascination of evil is most sharply focused
in the symbolic forms of Satan and the Antichrist,
as metaphorical expressions of a
malign power destructive of humanity.
— Rosemary Muir Wright

We do not know – John's Gospel is silent on this point – what Lazarus experienced or how he reacted following his re-suscitation by Jesus. Yet we can well imagine how dumbstruck the witnesses must have been when they saw Lazarus come forth from the tomb, still awkwardly draped in his funereal wrappings. In his play *Lazarus Laughed*, Eugene O'Neill depicts Lazarus as a man who has tasted death and now sees it for what it is: Lazarus begins to laugh, softly at first, and then so heartily that his profound asser-tion of joy becomes infectious and everyone begins to laugh:

Laugh with me!
Death is dead!
Fear is no more!
There is only life!
There is only laughter![40]

John assures us that this was not just a near-death experience; he has Jesus declare quite emphatically: "Lazarus is dead" (John 11:14). We are also told that this startling event had a polarizing effect on the onlookers: some put their faith in Jesus, while others, the chief priests and the Pharisees in particular, drummed up a scenario of fear by declaring that should news of this event get around, "the Romans will come and destroy both our holy place and our nation" (John 11:48).

Fear has figured prominently in the annals of human history down to the present, and despite all human, scientific and religious attempts to ward off evil – real or perceived – the defence mechanisms we rely on and the ingenious security systems we set up to protect our children and ourselves from harm never seem adequate. None of our best security systems – from the child-proof bottle of medication, the mandatory air bags in cars, the latest gun-control legislation, our federal economic watchdogs and safety nets, to the sophisticated security systems in our airports, schools and business computers – ever seem sufficient. Even the Church's official sanctions and censures no longer have the deterring effect they perhaps once did. Sooner or later, we are confronted with another menace, threat or crisis, against which we feel helpless and are ill-prepared to face. When the threat looms large enough and whole populations are involved, as with the outbreak of war or an epidemic, our collective sense of vulnerability becomes as tangible and pandemic as the threat or menace itself. This collective sense of vulnerability was clearly in evidence in the United States after the September 11, 2001, attack on the Pentagon in Washington and the Twin Towers in New York.

What must it have been like to live during the fourteenth century when the plague, known as the Black Death, engulfed nearly the whole of Europe, striking down almost half of its population? Sufferers from the disease developed flu-like symptoms such as fever and chills. Swellings in the groin, neck and armpits were charged with vile-smelling pus. Many also suffered from purple or red discolouration under the skin, internal bleeding, and bloody urine, diarrhea or vomiting. Stories are told of doctors and priests ministering to the victims in the morning and being dead by nightfall themselves. By the year 1348, the plague had galloped through Italy, France and southern Austria, and quickly spread to England, Ireland and the rest of northwest Europe, Scandinavia, and even remote Iceland. Historians are not sure how many people died. Until recently, the consensus was that between one-third and one-half of Europe's population died from the plague. More current studies by such scholars as Norman Cantor and John Aberth are inclined to push the number of deaths even higher. The Black Death was without question the greatest calamity in European history. Medieval observers were in no doubt that this horrifying disease was the worst visitation of an angry God since the Flood, and believed the end of the world was imminent. This plague alone killed 25 million people, three times more than were killed during World War I. The disease swept through Europe like flames through a dry pine forest. Cities were sealed off, farms were abandoned, economies crumbled, food shortages became desperate. The general populace was terrorized and succumbed to a very fatalistic view of life. With so much death around them, is it any wonder that late-medieval men and women believed that the Apocalypse would soon come to pass? To get an idea of the terror spread by this plague, try to imagine that every other person you see may be dead tomorrow or the next day. As one chronicler, Agnolo di Tura, who lost his five children to the plague in Siena, put it: "There was no one who wept for any death, for all awaited death. And so many died that all believed it was the end of the world."

I chose this one example of widespread menace and terrorization because of its remoteness in history, and also because it quickens our imagination. Yet we have only to consider the unspeakable atrocities of our own day to realize that Hell and its demonic powers are still very real. We have only to think about Auschwitz and the extermination, under the Nazi regime and its collaborators, of six million Jews, two-thirds of the total European Jewish population, and 5 million other individuals; the mass extermination and

113

so-called "ethnic cleansing" that have taken place in Cambodia, Rwanda and Kosovo; or the massive murder-suicide tragedies that have recently taken place in doomsday cults in Uganda, Guyana, France and the United States. But perhaps the closest "functional equivalent" of the Devil today is that most insidious and silent enemy called AIDS. To date the toll taken by this virus around the world is nearly 22 million dead, 36 million currently infected with HIV and AIDS, 13 million children orphaned as a result, another 15,000 people contracting the disease every day and, sadly, this being only about 40 per cent of the cases being reported world-wide. The magnitude of this raging epidemic has far exceeded even the worst predictions made by experts as recently as a decade ago. However represented in the Bible or in Christian iconography, and by whatever other name Satan may take on, has the Devil, this Prince of Darkness, ever evinced a more insidious and vicious presence in our day than the AIDS virus? Has he ever exercised his powers on a more worldwide, indiscriminate scale? Have his demonic powers, in the guise of this disease, ever been more contagious, more mysterious, or more focused on creating total devastation? In the end, is it really too difficult to imagine that the HIV/AIDS viruses are but another name for, another facet of, our traditional symbol of the Devil?

In her treatise *AIDS and Its Metaphors*, Susan Sontag brings together two powerful metaphors surrounding this disease. First, AIDS is depicted as an "invader": the enemy invades and destroys you from within. This fact then strengthens the use of military metaphors in medicine. The medical and public health response has been to "declare war" against AIDS, much like it did against cancer. Second, because AIDS is a sexually transmitted disease, it also harbours the theme plague-as-punishment. While Sontag herself strongly argues against the use of such metaphoric thinking, especially in her earlier work *Illness as Metaphor*, she never makes a convincing case as to why it is unhealthy to think metaphorically about illness. Metaphor is the normal and primordial vehicle of knowledge. In fact, imaginative thinking has always prevailed during times of great crisis, illness and conflict. The image of Death itself, ever present and unconquerable, has always inspired our greatest authors, artists and mystics. One thinks of the Dance of Death, or Danse Macabre, in François Villon's *Testament,* where he portrays life's fleeting pleasures; or Shakespeare's *Measure for Measure*; or Cervantes' *Don Quixote*. Even in modern times, the metaphor has endured, with, for instance Camille Saint-Saëns' musical tone poem *The Danse Macabre,* described in Hermann Hesse's novel *Narcissus and Goldmund* and played in the finale of Ingmar Bergman's film *The Seventh Seal.* The mystics, too, saw illness and death as powerful metaphors. Illness, for example, plays a significant role in *Showing of Love* by Julian of Norwich, where sickness is the genesis of her mysticism. She desired to be ill in order to re-enact Christ's suffering. For her, pain and suffering have a definite twofold purpose: on the one hand, they remind us of the passion of Christ; and on the other, they give us the opportunity for personal redemption, through which we come to know the everlasting love of God.

What is obvious is that metaphoric (imaginative) thinking is precisely the way in which we humans discover meaning in our lives, especially when we suffer or confront evil, and any serious thinking about evil or death without using metaphor is well-nigh impossible. Much time, talent and energy have been spent throughout history in an attempt to understand the *problem* of evil. While the problem of evil is as real today as it ever was, there is a growing consensus that evil is as much a *mystery* as a problem. This brings us to our main concern in this chapter, namely, how the imagination deals with the mystery of evil and suffering. We begin with a brief overview of how the classic symbol of evil, the Devil, has been variously imaged over the centuries and the theological significance this powerful symbol may still hold for us today.

The Metamorphosis of a Symbol

The Devil did not make his appearance in the earliest Christian iconography. Representations of the Devil in Christian art date from the sixth century, where they appear in church frescoes and on the margins of illuminated manuscripts of the Bible. There seems to have been a reluctance in the early Church to represent Satan in visual form: no such depiction appears in the art of the catacombs and Satan, although deemed dangerous, was nevertheless regarded as one of God's creatures, albeit a fallen creature not unlike our human race. When the Devil does make his appearance, it is in the form of a fallen angel with a well-proportioned human head, clawed fingernails and a seductive, ironic smile on his face. There are none of the grotesque deformities that we see the Devil take on in the iconography of later centuries. Early Christian art tended to depict the Devil as a handsome young man, no doubt recognizing the fact that evil is often something attractive, something that can easily tempt and seduce us as an "apparent" or "deceptive" good. The Devil is thus depicted more as a "fallen hero" than a horrifying, dreadful figure. He retains a human form well into the twelfth century, as can be seen in Michelangelo's depiction of The Temptation and The Fall of Adam and Eve in the Sistine Chapel.

A significant transformation takes place in the twelfth century. The Devil loses his seductive traits of earlier centuries and now becomes a hideous monster. The head of the medieval Devil is particularly remarkable: it is always enormous, deformed and takes on quasi-bestial traits reminiscent of the Gorgons in Greek mythology, those three frightful, snake-haired sisters with wings and claws who had the power to turn anyone who looked at them into stone. This "hybrid" transformation in Satan's image coincided with the Church's attempt to impress upon Christians that Satan is indeed *the* Evil One who excels in leading humans into temptation. It was assumed that a more terrifying representation of Satan would have greater shock value and would motivate the peasant masses to be virtuous. If love alone was not enough to make believers virtuous, then perhaps fear might help. Another reason for this change was that the peasant masses in the Middle Ages could not read or write. Hence, the art and decorations of church buildings took on great importance for them as a "book" of religious instruction that familiarized them with the text of the gospels and the Bible. However, since these biblical scenes and characters were displayed on high in the stained glass windows, portals and capitals of the churches, there was an obvious need for the viewer below to be able to clearly distinguish the characters depicted in them. Hence in deliberate contrast to Christ, the saints and angels, Satan was increasingly stripped of his human attributes and given a more conspicuous and repulsive profile.

Another significant change takes place in the thirteenth-century Gothic representations of Satan. With the increasing drama of the Roman Catholic liturgy and the proliferation of miracle and mystery plays performed in the churchyard and market place, Satan not only continued to provoke fear but now he also became a source of amusement, a figure to laugh at.[41] Aron Gurevich, the foremost Russian historian of medieval culture and society, describes well the commingling of popular and ecclesiastical culture: "Carnival," he says, "is a distinctive correlate of the serious culture present in it: it penetrates its substance and 'lowers it' for a short while, but not essentially. This 'lowering' assumes neither denial nor disregard, but a temporary overcoming of it through an inclusive inversion."[42] What Gurevich is saying is that the high and low culture of medieval society must not be seen or interpreted as two sharply divided styles of life, the one serious, the other carnivalesque; rather, the two cultures are internally linked and co-penetrate in the consciousness of medieval men and women. Thus to laugh or make fun of the Devil was, by inversion, simply another way of affirming his presence and reality. As Gurevich goes on to say: "The humorous and the frightful are interwoven in the figure of the devil."

When a papal edict in 1210 forbade the clergy to act on a public stage, the supervision and control of presenting these plays passed into the hands of town guilds and the laity. Among the changes that ensued, the vernacular language replaced the Latin, greater liberty was taken to insert scenes that were not from the Bible and popular culture gained greater currency. The forces of evil still loomed large in the medieval consciousness, but the perception of demons as the very incarnation of evil should not be exaggerated. There is ample evidence of caricature and parody in Gothic religious art. First and foremost, the forces of evil seem to be subjected to ridicule.[43] A good example of this is the Last Judgment sculpture on the central portal of Notre Dame Cathedral in Paris, where a good number of demons can be seen in its arch mouldings. One of them sits contentedly on the damned as upon his throne, while others serve as his footstool. The Devil of Notre Dame is bulky and fat, with two conspicuous sagging breasts. He is quite repugnant but by no means terrifying. The tendency to portray the Devil as amusing and ridiculous rather than as a terrifying figure continued well into the fourteenth century.

The same ironic treatment of evil can be seen in the gargoyles of the Middle Ages, those nightmarish heads that adorn the walls and rooftops of the medieval cathedrals in Europe. Apart from the practical purpose of spewing off the rain water that fell on the lead roofs of the cathedrals, these ugly and grotesque monsters served two functions. Their first religious purpose was to remind the faithful that there is another world peopled by monsters, demons and strange beasts, a world close to Hell which awaits all those who fall into sin. Their second purpose was to ward off other more terrifying devils and demons in an attempt to protect the sanctity of the church and place of worship. The idea was to ward off demons with other demons (not altogether unlike our popular practice today of using an effigy of an owl to ward off unwanted pigeons).

When one compares the perception and treatment of demons in the Middle Ages with those of the succeeding period, medieval art proper is seen as more restrained and laconic. With Hieronymus Bosch (c. 1450–1516), Pieter Brueghel (c. 1525–1569), Mathias Grünewald (c. 1470–1528), and indeed throughout the Renaissance, an uncommon fascination with Hell takes hold and fuels the artistic, literary and religious imagination. Death is now personified in skeletal forms, and demons acquire horns and tails. When the demons are not devouring and excreting their victims, they roast them on spits and fry them in pans. Indeed the torments of Hell are depicted with such vividness and in such realistic detail that little is left to the imagination. This hellish orgy of stark realism and "abominable fancy" is particularly in evidence in the preaching of the times. There was a general consensus in European Christianity that the damned would suffer not only mental but also physical torments. Robert Cardinal Bellarmine (1542–1621), the great even-handed scholar, defender of papal power and Doctor of the Church, provides a good example of this. His sermon on Hell delivered at University of Louvain in Belgium in 1574 is very typical of the times. In it, Bellarmine describes in graphic detail the various torments inflicted not only on the four inner faculties of the soul but also on the five external senses:

O miserable eyes, which will be terrified by the horrendous forms of demons, which will be tormented by the densest smoke, which will always be open to behold your miseries! O miserable ears, which will hear forever the scourges and blasphemies and the groaning of the wretched! O wretched nostrils, which will smell forever the stench of a most filthy place and of stinking bodies! O wretched bellies and mouths, which shall be tormented by everlasting starvation and hunger and intolerable thirst! O wretched members, which shall inhabit that well which vomits up sulphurous flames![44]

Seventy-two years later, in 1658, we find Richard Younge, a preacher at the parish church of Magherafelt in Northern Ireland, no less graphic in his description of the physical torments of Hell:

As the eyes shall be tormented with ugly and fearful sights, of ghastly spirits; the ears with hideous screeching, and crying out, howling and yelling like dragons; the tongue with drought and thirst, craving with the rich glutton in hell.... And the minde, that is filled with horror and ghastly terrors....We cannot hold our finger for one minute in scalding lead; but there both body and soul shall fry in everlasting flames, and be continually tormented by internal fiends.[45]

There was ample precedent for such imaginative descriptions of Hell, the most famous being Dante's *Inferno*, composed when the Renaissance era was just beginning and in the final years of the poet's life. Here we see images of life after death, imaginings of the torments of Hell, as reflections of our lives now. The *Divine Comedy* enshrines our deepest hopes and dreams, and expresses our greatest fears and nightmares. Although Dante's *Inferno* explores very explicitly the theme of divine retribution and justice, the poem's unrelenting descriptions, categorizations and analyses of sin and human evil abound and fascinate. Dante depicts the sinners' punishments in Hell as a grotesque mimicry of their sins on Earth. Even Dante's Lucifer is made to appear as a grotesque inversion of God in Heaven. With his three horrible faces, one looking straight ahead and the other two looking over his shoulders, Lucifer constitutes a perversion of the Trinity. Each of Lucifer's mouths chews on a sinner, tearing the victim to pieces but never quite killing the poor wretch. Dante's goal was not to be a teacher/

theologian but, as a poet, to stimulate our imagination by surrounding it only with known forms and familiar objects. Little by little, we yield to our companion-poet's vivid imagination, and we take up his prodigious voyage in the flesh, as though it were our very own.

From the end of the seventeenth century, the Devil quietly begins to slip out of the European mind, and only makes an appearance again at the end of the eighteenth century. His reappearance is due in large measure to the publication of Goethe's *Faust* – the mythical story of a diabolical pact, in which a man, bent on being "like God," sells his soul to Satan in exchange for immortality, knowledge or monetary gain. Satan now regains a human form, elegant and attractive to better deceive his adversary. In Delacroix's painting *Faust,* we see the Devil hovering over the earth like the Prince of the World. With his large black wings, amply deployed, and a plume stuck in his lordship's felt hat, the Devil's figure is now pretty well etched on canvas and will henceforth be so imitated by other artists.

Today, we think of the devil quite differently, if we think of him at all.[46] Many would argue that belief in the existence of demons and the devil has now largely declined and, except for some fundamentalists and conservative Christian groups, few regret the disappearance of demons in the way they were imagined and visually depicted in the past. "Our" Satan is not identical with the Satan of the Middle Ages, nor are "our" demons identical with those of the Renaissance. People living in different historical periods have constructed different images of the devil corresponding to their religious sensibilities, just as the image of Christ has undergone changes throughout the centuries, and people have found in these representations various elements to value. All artistic and literary representations of the devil (like those of God) are invariably recast and re-imaged, often unconsciously, by later generations. This is made possible because of the extraordinary "surplus of meaning" encoded in any given symbol. Hence no past symbolic depiction of the devil, and no current evaluation of it, can simply be handed on to future generations without it somehow being modified, perhaps unrecognizably, in the process.

The changes in the symbolic representations of the devil over the centuries are an indication of this. What is important in evaluating these changes is how the people of another age imaged the devil and, more importantly, how these depictions must always be appreciated in the light of the religious sensibilities of the time. What motivated them? What was their vision of Christian faith fully lived? What role did this vision play in their lives and how did their efforts relate to their behaviour? To answer these critical questions requires an ability to imaginatively identify with people of another age, to transpose ourselves into a different age with all its particular social, political and religious circumstances, to see how we ourselves might have reacted and imagined the devil. With sufficient historical empathy, we can learn something not just about people of another age but also something about ourselves.

There is another important consideration to bear in mind. The symbolic representations of the devil, in any age, are just that: *symbolic representations*. Were the image or the understanding of the devil to remain forever fixed and unchanged in the minds of believers, that would be a sure sign that this erstwhile living symbol had lost its power to motivate and mobilize, that it had degenerated into a purely notional sign and decorative motif. Eric Voegelin is quite right when he says that the degradation and demise of symbols – even religious symbols – takes place when a symbol becomes detached from the human experience that first engendered it. The symbol becomes meaningless and is then merely understood as a language text "containing" its own precise meaning and nothing more. When this happens, Voegelin says, "the symbols may cease altogether to be translucent for reality."[47] In other words, they no longer open up levels of consciousness about the mystery of human existence, including the mystery of evil. The real power of symbols lies in their ability to speak deeply to people's experience. And when a symbol is wrenched from that experience, it no longer retains its power. By their nature, as we said earlier, symbols have the ability to simultaneously hold in creative tension a wide variety of both positive and negative meanings. Symbols do mean something; yet because of their inclusive and polyvalent nature they are always capable of meaning something more, something other. It is precisely because of their surplus of meaning that symbols can never be exhausted in any one given interpretation, however dogmatically defined or artistically rendered. If the main function of a symbol – including that of the devil – is to embrace (not define) the mystery of human existence and reality, then all attempts to pin down its meaning too precisely must be avoided.

It is my contention that belief in the devil today, those "principalities and powers" of evil of which the Bible speaks, is just as "real" in our Western consciousness as in any other age. Is not the unspeakable horror of the recent terrorist attacks on the World Trade Center and the Pentagon sufficient to remind everyone the world over that demonic forces still lurk faceless in the midst of our civilized world? "Beyond comprehension," "beyond our wildest imaginings," "beyond belief" – this is how people struggled to describe the events of that fateful Tuesday morning. We still live within this classic symbol of evil, but we experience and "read" it differently. The experiences of evil in our present-day consciousness, whether the evil is physical or moral, in the psychic life of the individual or in society, are not only very real but they also constitute a "functional equivalent" of any primordial experience of evil that Adam and Eve may have had, or that Job experienced on his heap of ashes or that Jesus suffered on the cross. The devil is very "real" for us today, even though he has taken on a cunningly altered guise and now assumes a new name. The presumed modern-day demise of the devil is itself deceptive. There are those who would argue that belief in the existence of the devil has all but vanished in our technological age. Many believe that the devil has lost his grip on the minds of Western Christians. As one anthropologist has put it: "Christians in the West have gone beyond renouncing the devil; they practically deny his existence."[48] But is this really the case? Has the devil really vanished from our Western consciousness? Or is such a judgment perhaps not based on the mistaken view that living symbols, like absolute truths, must always be interpreted in exactly the same way? There are also some respected theologians, like Karl Rahner, who believe that the role of the devil can and perhaps should be legitimately downplayed; that it is pastorally feasible to explain the truths of faith today "even without explicit teaching about the devil." And Rahner adds:

"We must very definitely avoid drawing on the traditional arsenal of popular pictures of the devil."[49]

So what are we to make of all this? It is safe to say that the refusal to "overrate" the devil falls well within the very best Christian tradition and that the refusal to "underrate" the devil is no less genuinely Christian. Yet in order to appreciate the devil as a symbolic reality with its remarkable and enduring vitality in today's world, we must turn our attention to the role which the imagination plays in this whole devilish affair.

The Theological Function of the Imagination

It is our religious imagination that keeps the symbol of the devil alive and securely anchored in our everyday human awareness of evil. This might be its most important theological function: it prevents our religious symbols from being wrenched from our lived experience and thus keeps them from drifting into forgetfulness or oblivion. It prevents the sinister supra-human power of evil from ever being completely glossed over or trivialized. It is the imagination, more than anything else, that gives power to religious symbols, including those of the devil – the power, that is, to construe reality in dimensions that far exceed its "showing" or empirical appearance. As theologian Roger Haight puts it:

> The imagination, by projecting and injecting deeper meaning into reality, also discovers dimensions that are already there. In their turn symbols evoke sets of meaning that genuinely illumine reality; they shed light on and reveal dimensions otherwise invisible. In sum, symbols bestow meaning on the external world by allowing human beings *to see with their imagination* what would otherwise remain hidden.[50]

The first thing the imagination does for any symbol, including the demonic symbol of evil, is to safeguard its enigmatic and intentionally ambiguous quality. It prevents us from trivializing evil and thinking that it is but another human problem to be solved rather than a mystery that envelops us at every turn. Imagination preserves the enigma of evil as a *question* – not so much in the abstract such as "Why does evil exist?" but the more searing personal question: "Why *this* particular evil? Why *me*? Why must *my* innocent child die?" Such questions of evil and suffering, especially when visited upon the just and the innocent, can never be satisfactorily answered. And it is left to our tantalizingly "wild" imagination to see to it that the question of evil is never stifled, never prematurely foreclosed, never given a definitive, authoritative answer. A good illustration of this mystery is found in the Book of Job. As Paul Ricoeur reminds us, even here the enigmatic and perhaps deliberately ambiguous character of evil is preserved. No direct reply is given to Job's repeated questions concerning personal suffering. What we have instead is the vision of a Creator whose designs are unfathomable. Confronted by such a mystery, the imagination may suggest any number of possible scenarios, but it never eliminates the question, much less the mystery, of evil. Is Job's consolation to be deferred until after his death? Or is Job's complaint misguided, even set aside, in the eyes of God, the ruler over life and death? Or is this uncertainty perhaps something that Job must endure as a purification so that he can love God "for naught" in response to Satan's wager at the beginning of the story? Who can say with any real certainty? The bedeviling thing about all such searing questions about evil is that we all experience them, in varying degrees of intensity, in our own lives. When visited personally by some evil, whether it be a stroke, a heart attack or the misfortune of being prematurely laid off work, who can claim never to have experienced Job's quandary?

The evils once attributed to the devil – sickness of body or mind, great epidemics, failure of crops and the like – are today viewed quite differently. It is also true that in our modern age we have a pronounced tendency to value hard facts and data over realities that are not scientifically verifiable. Yet notwithstanding this bias, the human imagination is forever drawing us into the vortex of mystery – and keeping us there! This is what it does best. Divine revelation conveys the Evil One to us in mythical and symbolic form: Satan is a fallen angel; a superior spiritual power with consciousness and intention; immutably fixed in opposition to everything good, beautiful and holy; the implacable enemy of God and us humans. This ultimate symbol of evil is kept alive through the imagination, and therefore the symbol is able to reveal some important truths about evil (and ourselves) that we would otherwise miss or overlook. What are some of these truths encoded in the demonic symbol? Among them, John Macquarrie suggests, is "the depth and mystery of evil; the superhuman dimensions of evil; its sometimes apparently systemic character; and the fact that a spiritual nature is no safeguard against evil and may indeed issue in the worst forms of evil."[51]

Whenever we experience the danger or frightening prospect of evil, such as the loss of our child or our health, the demonic symbol comes into play and suddenly our hold on life and everything we hold dear appears in serious jeopardy. The futility of all our past good intentions, our best human efforts and securities, suddenly appears very real. We have a sense that we are no longer in control, that our life is not completely ours to decide and that perhaps there is much more at stake here than we had hitherto led ourselves to believe. It is at this precise moment of grace – albeit a grace in terrible disguise – that our imagination draws us deeper into the mystery of evil. We become conscious of our contingency and our dependence upon some mysterious forces beyond our reckoning. Are these powers diabolical or divine, maleficent or beneficent – or are they perhaps conspiring against me in some sort of unthinkable collusion? Is my suffering and the death of my child a punishment? Is there perhaps not a connection between the sins that I have committed and the physical or moral evil that is now being visited upon me? Could it be that there *is* such a thing as an ancestral dimension to evil, that reparation for past sins and injustices must be made by later generations? And do I not also feel like an innocent victim in precisely what is now making me feel guilty? Here again, even at the limit of despair and death, the mystery of evil and its opaqueness are preserved intact. It is precisely in and out of the vortex of this abiding mystery that Christian hope is born, that sufficient space is created in the believer for an unqualified hope in the risen Lord – and, if necessary, as St. Paul insists, even a "hope against hope."

If the first theological function of the imagination consists in drawing us ineluctably, if unwittingly, into the mystery of evil, its second function is to "keep" us there as long as possible. We give a name to our demons *today* as in every age: militarism, ethnic cleansing, genocide, racism, hate crimes, sexism, etc. These all appear to us as horrifying patches of darkness, "works" of the devil that, as Christians, we promised to renounce at baptism. Unfortunately, one of the ways we are prone to "renounce" them is to turn our backs on them, to shut our eyes tightly to them, to have nothing to do with them. There are many ways to eschew the "works and pomps" of the devil, but perhaps there is none more un-Christlike than to turn a blind eye to them. But the imagination will have none of this! It rebels against the head-in-the-sand responses we sometimes make in the face of glaring injustices. Even when the demonic powers take on a new name and a new guise, the imagination keeps them well before our eyes. How does it do this? With what ploys does it conjure up our "awakening"? In order to prevent us from making evil invisible, from "vaporizing" it − out of sight, out of mind! − the imagination keeps the mesmerizing power of evil inescapably within and before us. We see this particularly in our inherent fascination with evil. Our present-day fascination with evildoing, violence, cruelty and injustice of every description is evident in the way we assiduously follow the latest scandal on the nightly news and in our newspapers and magazines. The spectre of evildoing and violence is clearly a commodity that "sells," and it sells precisely because it continues to enchant, bewitch, seduce and fascinate us − by the very same beguiling traits that have been traditionally attributed to the Devil, the Great Tempter. It should be pointed out here, as noted in an earlier chapter, that the "way" of the imagination is one of seduction and beguilement. This no doubt explains why the Church has so often mistrusted the imagination: on the surface, at least, its seductive *modus operandi* can be mistaken for the wiles and ways of the Devil, the Great Tempter.

Our fascination with the devil (evil) has by no means disappeared. Just look at how the recent low-budget horror movie *The Blair Witch Project* gripped the American pop consciousness, reminiscent of other films such as *The Exorcist, Rosemary's Baby* and *The Mephisto Waltz*. These and other movies generated some of the highest profits in film history. Clearly, the "fascination with evil" is a phenomenon that runs deep in both the social and religious spheres of our everyday lives. The prestigious theological journal *Concilium*, which began in 1964 during the Vatican Council and whose founders included such well-known theologians as Yves Congar, J.B. Metz and Edward Schillebeeckx, even saw fit to make our human penchant and fascination with evil the central theme of a recent issue.[52] All ten contributors wrestled with and brilliantly exposed some aspect or other of this phenomenon. From a perspective that was critical of culture, society and religion, each contributor put forward the cautious hope that ways may be found to overcome this pernicious fascination. The authors were right in appealing to Christian hope, but they were unable to offer any serious or concrete suggestions or practical remedies for overcoming this fascination with evil. Is this yet another sign that people's fascination with evil is here to stay and that, in a real sense, it is a humanly *inescapable* phenomenon? Could it also be that our instinctual fascination with evil, which the imagination certainly fuels, has at least one important "saving grace," namely, the ability to save us from what James Hillman calls the "anesthetized heart"? Hillman means a heart that demonstrates little or no reaction to what it faces or beholds — including the horrendous outbreaks of evil we witness all around us. He is describing a heart that becomes so indifferent to evil that it turns the real face of the world into monotony, oneness and "more-of-the-same." And is this not one of the devil's traditional wiles: to anesthetize and make us numb to the evil before us?

It could be argued (and I am making the claim here) that in fuelling our fascination with evil, the imagination assumes something of the role formerly played by the "devil's advocate" in the Church's processes of beatification and canonization.

The Devil's Advocate was the popular term given to the Promoter of the Faith, an official of the Congregation of Rites at the Vatican, whose business it was to scrupulously examine all the evidence, both of miracles and virtue, about a candidate whose cause was being presented for beatification or canonization. The activities of this official promoter of the faith were to raise questions, cast doubts or otherwise argue against a case if the evidence was warranted. Thus the old system was modelled on a legal trial, with the arguments of a postulator (the official who presents a plea for the beatification or canonization of a person) being weighed and argued against by the promoter of the faith. Today, of course, the process has been streamlined, and the position of the Devil's Advocate has been eliminated. Kenneth L. Woodward astutely points out in his work *Making Saints* that the abuses by the Devil's Advocate were factors in the elimination of this official's role in the process of canonization in 1983.[53] Gone are the lawyers and many of the time-consuming legal quibbles, posturing and heated courtroom scenes. The updated rules place a greater emphasis on a historical rather than a legal approach, and a candidate's sanctity is viewed more in the light of his or her response to the challenges of a particular time and place rather than against some universal, timeless prototypes of sanctity.

Although the office of the Devil's Advocate was abolished in 1983, his seemingly negative role did have a positive value, inasmuch as it prevented the Church from declaring someone a saint too precipitously (without sufficient examination of the cause in question) or from being too easily seduced by public opinion or enthusiasm. It also compelled those promoting the cause to be more diligent and thorough in their investigation of the candidate's worthiness to receive the Church's highest honour. Similarly, the imagination assumes the role of the Devil's Advocate by keeping us awake and alert to the reality of evil, and by not allowing us to become careless, insensitive or numb to the atrocious injustices in our world. When the imagination assumes this role, we become uncomfortable, even fearful. Fear of the devil and fear of the imagination seem always to have coincided and overlapped at some point. When the imagination fuels our fascination with evil, there is no longer a place to hide. Sooner or later we are obliged to come to our senses, sit up and take notice, even though, reluctantly, we are obliged to give up our dreamlike complacency before the spectre of evil. To remain neutral or indifferent is no longer a tenable option. And the defining moment arrives when the question is raised: "What stand must I personally take in the face of *this* evil?"

I call this a "defining" moment advisedly because it is at this point that the religious character of the imagination becomes more evident and explicit. As the imagination nudges us into higher awareness, we are no longer mere onlookers or impartial bystanders to evil, and the transcendent reality of sin now begins to tug at our Christian conscience. Like Adam and Eve who had no place to hide their nakedness after the Fall, we now feel implicated in "knowing" sin. It is to this third theological function of the imagination we now turn.

In the Christian scheme of things, the reality of sin is a revealed truth and a mystery. And like so many other revealed truths, sin in the Bible is presented to us mythically. From the opening chapters of the Book of Genesis, we read:

> They [Adam and Eve] heard the sound of the Lord God walking in the garden at the time of the evening breeze, and the man and his wife hid themselves from the presence of the Lord God among the trees of the garden. But the Lord God called to the man, and said to him, "Where are you?" He said, "I heard the sound of you in the garden, and I was afraid, because I was naked; and I hid myself." He said, "Who told you that you were naked?" (3:8-11)

In this telling story, as in so many others, divine revelation is depicted not only as a matter of God's emergence from obscurity but also as our coming out of hiding into the presence of God. What this myth tells us is that revelation is not merely a unilateral self-disclosure on the part of God but is a reciprocal self-disclosure, a mutual unveiling. God reveals himself to us in the very act of our coming out of hiding. Expressed in mythical form, sin is depicted as our strange need to hide – in this instance from God, but elsewhere in the Bible, from one another – and, indeed, not infrequently from ourselves. We often deceive ourselves with respect both to what constitutes our true happiness and to what prevents it. The mystery of human iniquity, under whatever guise and regardless of the prime instigator, always entails a "cover up" of sorts, some attempt to hide or keep something secret. Did this not become tragically and painfully evident in the recent abuse scandal in the Roman Catholic archdiocese of Boston, as well as President Clinton's earlier White House scandal and testimony? This explains in part why people continue to be so fascinated by the public exposure of any sordid affair in the private lives of the rich and the powerful. Nor can there be any doubt that the media are only too eager to capitalize on this "hide-and-seek" syndrome. But more to the point: the mystery of evil implicates us all, and sooner or later, like Adam and Eve, we become conscious of our own nakedness, poverty and vulnerability.

Before this little miracle – called "conversion" in traditional Christian spirituality – takes place, we think we are freed and liberated only because we are very forgetful: we forget about the log that is in our own eye and gloat over the speck that is in our neighbour's (Matthew 7:3). Jesus' speech mode not only appeals to the theological imagination but sends it on its unrelenting quest to probe and "uncover" some further connections encoded in the symbolization of sin and evil. The reader will recall that one of the special gifts of the imagination is its intuitive ability to divine connections between things that appear at first sight to be unrelated and, therefore, usually go unnoticed or undetected (Chapter 4). With this uncanny gift, the theological imagination seeks out hidden connections that might otherwise be overlooked. In this case, it exposes and brings into sharper focus the hidden interconnections, collusion and complicity, for example, between Third World poverty, big business and the recent policy of globalization, and how we are all, however indirectly, implicated in the plight of the world. Whenever the imagination lights on such a connection, we are faced with another paradox, another point of tension. Let us now take a closer look at some of these more insidious connections.

The religious imagination has always divined a connection, first of all, between the "past" and the "present" in the power of sin. Instead of seeing sin as merely an individual affair, the religious imagination has always been fascinated by its trans-historical character. The myth of "original sin" is the child of this fascination. Through this myth, the religious imagination uncovers and exposes a sinful solidarity between the past and the present, a tensive connection between the sins of our forebears and our own. The power of sin is imagined as a trans-generational human phenomenon, something that is mysteriously passed on to those yet unborn, something that is contagious by its very nature and handed down from one generation to the next. This explanation of sin, of course, flies in the face of reason and has always "bedeviled" theologians who try to explain the myth of original sin in purely rational terms. Yet the religious imagination refuses to let this myth die and stubbornly prevents the reality of sin and evil from becoming too readily "privatized." Even the Church recognizes this today, as seen in John Paul's historic plea for forgiveness for the sins of Christians throughout history. We also see it in the reparations that are being demanded for injustices and abuses that occurred in the distant past, so distant, in fact, that we scarcely remember or have first-hand knowledge of them.

Along with this connection between the past and the present, the religious imagination is also quick to "see" in the mystery of sin a paradoxical connection between human freedom and bondage, a connection in which wilfulness and powerlessness are joined in an "unholy" alliance. For all the rational sophistication that psychologists, social analysts and theologians bring to bear on this enigma, the paradox of sin remains. The religious imagination stubbornly refuses to let the mystery of sin be explained away. At sin's very core it "sees" a connection wherein the voluntary and the involuntary co-penetrate, where freedom and bondage embrace. This explains why, on the one hand, we can identify so deeply with St. Paul's inner conflict when he says, "I do not do the good I want, but the evil I do not want is what I do" (Romans 7:19), and on the other hand, why our faithful imagination is quick to unmask our involvement and complicity in sin. Hence the paradox: sin is perceived simultaneously as something self-inflicted and as something "visited" upon us. When the Christian prays for forgiveness it is not only for his or her deliberate sins but also for that deeper complicity in sin which is both "mine" and "not mine." The imagination, as mentioned earlier, like the symbols it fuels, unites and keeps in creative tension those realities that seem contradictory or mutually exclusive. It eschews the either/or dualism to which we have become accustomed and fosters, instead, a unitary vision of reality. And it does this by uncovering the hidden and more obscure alliances that can so easily go undetected, ignored or repressed.

Another connection envisaged by the religious imagination, one that liberation theology has highlighted to its great credit, is that between "personal" sin and what is now called "structural" sin or "sinful social structures." The inability on the part of many Christians to think of social structures as being sinful is perhaps yet another sign of the devil's insidious nature. Evil can and does insinuate itself, surreptitiously and beyond any individual's personal responsibility, into some of our most hallowed institutions and social structures. Even the Church's ecclesiastical structures are not immune from this danger. It is not my intention to discuss or even attempt to theologically justify structural sin. I simply wish to point out that the religious imagination refuses to be restrained by any time-honoured definition of sin and is forever suggesting new ways of understanding and speaking about it. Again, the religious imagination assumes the role of the Devil's Advocate and would thwart any attempt to "domesticate" the mystery of evil by encapsulating the notion of sin in a clear concept or manageable moral definition.

The theological imagination does not and never will produce a *definitive* theology of sin, such as we inherited from the scholastic school of thought in which everything is clearly defined and spelled out. Sin was there defined as a deliberate transgression of a law of God by a responsible person when he or she knew it was wrong or forbidden by God. To be serious or mortal, a sin had to involve a grievous matter, done with sufficient reflection or advertence to its being clearly and indubitably forbidden by God, and deliberately done anyway. In contrast to this sort of clinical precision and rational definition, the theological imagination offers a much more *suggestive* and indeed more *awesome* notion of sin. It does not presume to reduce the mystery of evil to an exact science, and in this respect, it is always ready to give the devil his due! It always prepares us to be surprised and subjected to yet another new "in-breaking" of evil in our world, no less than the "in-breaking" of God's rule and reign in our midst. Both come as a surprise, unforeseen and unexpected – the one as temptation to sin and the other as unsolicited grace.

In matters so mysterious and startling, experience counts for more than doctrine. Experience tells us a certain obscurity sometimes sheds more light than excessive clarity. This is especially true in the religious domain because, as indicated earlier, God sings some of his most beautiful songs in the night. And when he does sing, it behooves the religious imagination to pay close attention and, when necessary, to create a new word, a new syntax and new lyrics to express the "unthinkable" and the "unimaginable." As though underscoring our linguistic and doctrinal poverty, the theological imagination prompts us to invent new terms which invariably jar our conventional sensibilities. In short, *the religious imagination affirms the right of new words to be born.* When they make their first appearance in the Church, however, such linguistic creations are generally viewed with great skepticism, if not with downright censorship. Yet historically, this has always been the case. Theology and the development of dogma would never have been possible without some new utterance, some new words added to the Church's lexicon. In any tradition, new words are as subversive as they are prophetic because they often inaugurate a new "order" of things. Not only can words determine and pin down meaning (that is their primary function), but as linguistic symbols, new words also suggest new ways of re-visioning conventional ideas, new ways of walking together into the future, indeed new ways of discerning the more recent incursions of the devil into our world as well as the new "in-breaking" of God's reign in our midst. Perhaps it is our lack of religious imagination that has prevented us from realizing that both Satan *and* the kingdom of God are closer at hand than we realize.

7

Under the Shadow of the Gods

The gods are personifications
of the energies that inform life —
the very energies that are building the trees
and moving the animals
and whipping up the waves of the ocean.
The very energies that are in your body
are personified by the gods.
They're alive and well in everybody's life.
— Joseph Campbell

If the devil has been portrayed as the principal instigator of evil in the tradition and popular piety of the Church, an equally ominous threat for the Church have been the "other gods" with whom the Church has had to compete since the beginning of its existence. The God of Abraham, Isaac and Jacob, the God of Jesus

Christ, never seems to have been very tolerant on this score. Nor is it surprising that the three great monotheistic religions – Judaism, Islam and Christianity – share a similar, almost paranoiac aversion to "other gods." When Christianity became the official state religion of the Roman Empire, it preached an exclusively monotheistic doctrine that excluded, and was hostile to, the polytheistic imagination. The Church required an either/or choice of belief systems: either many gods and goddesses were recognized and worshipped, or there was only one divine being and personal God, "the One" which is the source of all creation. A person could not have it both ways since the one belief was thought to cancel out the other – or so it appeared in an overly literalist reading of things. One could not simultaneously be a monotheist *and* a polytheist. Because of our rational Western bias, moreover, we have been unable to comfortably deal with mythical figures and their wild stories and outrageous adventures. We regard them as figments of an imagination gone wild, and we dismiss them outright in the belief that they simply could not be literally true. And literalism, as we know, stifles the sense of mystery and reduces the multiplicity of meanings to one uniform definition. Literalism, it has been suggested, is the natural result of the monotheistic tendency to demand singleness of meaning which hardens the heart, the seat of imagination, and prevents us from appreciating any wisdom that the ancient gods and goddesses might have offered us.

Add to this difficulty the fact that early Western anthropologists had their own *a priori* assumptions (read: "bias") about these two belief systems. They generally regarded and heralded monotheism as a "higher," "more advanced" or "superior" form of belief. Throughout the nineteenth century, historians regarded these ancient pagan mythologies as at best a natural, innate proclivity for the absolute, a sort of "larval precursor" of the one supreme God, a seed that foreshadowed and prepared the way for belief in the one true God of history. In the twentieth century, especially between the 1920s and 1940s, this somewhat "spiritualistic" school of interpretation was challenged by the more "positivistic" historians of religion. Martin P. Nilsson, for example, took what he believed was a more "common sense" approach to paganism; he reckoned that paganism should be understood from the perspective of those living in the country and therefore closer to nature, as opposed to the more sophisticated city dweller. He was at least correct as far as the etymological meaning of the word "pagan" is concerned, for it originally referred to a country dweller – perhaps with the slight disparaging connotation of a country bumpkin or a socially inept person. In this same context, it is also interesting to note that the word "heathen," which the *Oxford Dictionary* defines as "a person not belonging to a predominant religion, esp. not a Christian, Jew or Muslim," derives from the word "heath" which, not unlike the word "pagan," denotes a tract of uncultivated land overgrown with shrubs. Others, like Walter F. Otto, were more subtle in their approach to other religions, and tried to show how each god or goddess represented a special sphere of human existence, a somewhat exemplary experience of what it means for humans living in this world. Later, in the 1960s and under the influence of the noted Georges Dumézil, historians and anthropologists began taking a closer look not so much at the individual deities in and of themselves but at their forming a complex web of *relationships* said to exist between the gods. They utilized a "structural" form of analysis and sought to see where and how the gods and goddesses complemented one another, to what extent they opposed one another and where they appeared in the hierarchy within which we find them variously located in the known pantheons and shrines dedicated to "several" gods. Yet for all this scholarly research and study, it is still difficult for us to think of polytheism as harbouring anything of real value. We still tend to look upon such a belief system as sheer "vanity and nothingness," to borrow an Old Testament expression.

Our difficulty in understanding how the Greeks and the Romans, two otherwise great civilizations from whom we have inherited so much, could possibly believe in so many gods is probably due to the historical decline and virtual disappearance of polytheism in our own Western world. Its historical and geographical remoteness from anything we have known or experienced virtually precludes a fair assessment of what was actually involved in this belief system. It simply does not fall within our daily existence or present-day experience. Our difficulty is further compounded by the fact that we have generally lost our ability to deal with myths, something that is crucial if we want to do justice to polytheistic thinking and imagining of the past. For us today, a myth is something unreal, a figment of one's imagination, with no objective foundation in reality. The significance of myths and mythmaking almost completely escapes our modern empirical way of thinking. Yet this is the way Joseph Campbell, an acknowledged scholar of myths and mythmaking, sums up their benefit and what myths can do for us – if we would only allow them to function properly. First, they can awaken and maintain in us a sense of awe and gratitude as regards the mysterious dimension of the world we live in. Second, a living mythology offers us an image of the universe that mirrors and is in keeping with our knowledge of the times. Third, myths serve to validate, support and inform the moral norms of the society in which we live. And fourth, they guide us, stage by stage, in health, strength and harmony of spirit "through the whole foreseeable course of a useful life."[54] Teilhard de Chardin perhaps best expressed our modern difficulty in dealing with myths when he said that "in contrast to the 'primitives,' who gave a face to everything that moves, or the early Greeks who deified every aspect and all the forces of Nature, modern man is obsessed by the need to depersonalize all that he most admires."[55]

Unless one is a scholar interested in such remote things, it is difficult to develop a "listening heart" for the gods and goddesses of old who have all but fallen silent to us. Or have they really? In this chapter, I wish to take a closer look at what is being called the "return" of the gods and goddesses, how they are again making their presence felt to a growing number of people today and what role the imagination might be playing in this return of the "other gods" at the turn of this new century. But before focusing on the emerging "new" polytheism, some preliminary remarks are in order concerning the nature of polytheism as it existed in our Western world before its demise. This may help to dispel some of our misconceptions and misinformation about what polytheism entailed as a belief system and what it can possibly mean for us today, and may also shed light on why these gods and goddesses of old are still capable of fascinating us today.

Polytheism Revisited

The first corrective we must make in our understanding of polytheism concerns the nature of these ancient gods and goddesses and how they were looked upon in the ancient world. We should not think of them as representing a multiplicity of divine "persons" (as we understand the notion of person today).

To be sure, when we read about them in Greek or Roman mythology, or when they turn up in the poems of the nineteenth- and twentieth-century poets, they come across as real and distinctive characters, in much the same way that Shakespeare's characters appear real. There is a consistency in their profiles, an aggregate of qualities, an unquestionable "conspicuousness" about them that enables us to distinguish one character from another. In Greek mythology, for example, Ajax could even recognize Poseidon by his gait, even though the latter was disguised as Calchas. He saw him from behind and knew it was Poseidon "from his feet, his legs." In short, character is what distinguishes the gods and sets them off from one another. In the same way that Macbeth is not Hamlet, so Orpheus is not Apollo. This also explains why these characters are capable of "captivating" us and holding our attention though they are not, for all that, real persons.

So who are these strange pagan gods? What do they represent? They represent first and foremost many differentiated forces in nature and in society. They represent the powerful and sometimes capricious forces at work in the cosmic, social, political and ritual order of human life. In this pluralistic system of representations, the Greek gods and goddesses never establish or entertain real, direct and personal relationships with their devout believers – in contrast to what we believe in our monotheistic religions. Their relations with mortals are always mediated through society. Generally speaking, the Greek deities are only represented as having relations between themselves, and even this commerce is depicted in anthropomorphic terms, i.e., much like what takes place between human beings. In Roman mythology and religion, however, this inter-deity commerce is virtually absent. With their highly developed sense of order and efficiency, the Romans viewed their gods much more in terms of their different functions and types of actions. Just as the world is experienced in a variety of ways, so there are many specialized gods: some of a local nature (gods of specific localities, cities, roads; household gods of hearth and home) and some of a more obvious functional nature (gods of hunting and fishing; gods of specific arts, trades and crafts; gods of illness, cure, fertility, agriculture, etc.). To give but one example: the Greek God Zeus was essentially an anthropomorphic "personification" of the animate sky. He was mainly associated with the atmosphere and its phenomena, notably storms and other meteorological events like thunder and lightning and he performed his actions either in the sky or on the summit of mountains. He was often spoken of as the sky itself, sometimes bright and sunny, sometimes rainy and ominous. It was in this dual capacity that Zeus was revered, invoked and feared. Like the other gods of the Greek pantheon, Zeus was very powerful, but he was not omnipotent. Nor was he ever regarded as the Creator of either the celestial realm or the universe. Although Zeus is often depicted as above all the other gods, he is only one among equals, a *primus inter pares*, and Greek mythology clearly shows him to be limited and often held in check by the other gods.

Polytheism was a pluralistic system of representations and, as such, did not possess or entertain a supreme, overarching divine figure. Although the major deities were powerful – and indeed some were said to be more powerful than others – no one god was "omnipotent," "all-knowing" or "all-powerful" (as the monotheism of ancient Israel and Islam regarded their God). Polytheism was also an open belief system. It could receive or incorporate any new force or power that it encountered. This flexibility can be seen, for example, in the high degree of religious tolerance that existed in the polytheistic belief system. The Romans and Greeks never doubted the power and strength of their warring enemy, and they made every effort to discover and befriend these powers once they had defeated their adversaries in battle. When victorious in battle, the conquerors would take the foreign statues as prisoners in the belief that, henceforth, they could learn and benefit from the enhanced power taken from their enemy. It is also quite remarkable that there never was a religious war between the pagans, unlike the many wars waged by the different monotheistic religions throughout history.

The powers in question were the life forces and cosmic powers that make up human life here on Earth. The ancient Greeks and Romans represented these in figural form, as so many individualized deities, each with its own proper name and imaged form and function. In the same way that we give a name and precise meaning to various forms of violence in our society (e.g., hate crimes, genocide, racial prejudice, sexism, structural violence, wife or child abuse, etc.), so the ancient Greeks differentiated various forms of aggression under the godly names of Pan, Athena, Ares and Artemis/Apollo. Among their many mythical stories that differentiated the many faces of violence, the goddess Athena, whose function it was to protect the city, always fought defensively, much as our firefighters today seek to save homes in the face of fires that have gone out of control. Her style of warfare was not that of Ares, who loved to fight just for the sake of fighting, not unlike the modern-day mercenary. But even Ares was never as earthy and irrational as Pan, whom the soldiers invoked for luck in battle. Artemis and Apollo, on the other hand, formed an adolescent team but with none of the violent sophistication that characterized either Athena or Ares. And even Apollo, we are told, would eventually suffer sufficiently to outgrow his violent nature.

In much the same way that the Bible speaks anthropomorphically of God – how the Lord has eyes that can see, ears that can hear, a voice that can be heard, a heart that can relent and forgive – similarly, but inversely, the ancient Greeks and Romans attributed divine qualities to human, social and cosmic realities. The term "theomorphic" does in fact exist in our dictionary – meaning "having the likeness or form of God" – but it was seldom if ever used in reference to these pagan gods. This is a pity and says something about the monotheistic bias in our Western culture and vocabulary. We are quite prepared to accept that the Bible speaks of the Lord in an anthropomorphic manner, but find it difficult to imagine how the Greeks and the Romans could speak of cosmic realities in a theomorphic manner, that is, "as if" they were divine. We readily accept metaphoric speech in our monotheistic religion, and are quick to ascribe only the most literal meaning to polytheistic thinking. Within such a framework, the "One" alone could be divine, not the "many."

In sum, polytheistic thinking represents an attempt by society to articulate its understanding of the cosmos and of the superior powers that govern it, and to structure its relationship with these powers within an appropriate mythological system. These mythologies were not only attempts to explain the origin of things; they were also an appropriate way to understand and validate things as they were, or appeared to be, in those earlier times – things cosmic, social, political or ritual, as the case may be. We can now safely say that, in general, these polytheistic systems were an elaborate system of classification of those powers that were both within and beyond our human control. They were also mythical modes of thinking that readily lent themselves to various ways of conceiving and organizing society. No wonder that Cicero could say: "The gods attend to important matters and neglect small ones" – so unlike the Judeo-Christian God for whom "even the hairs of your head are counted" (Luke 12:7). Indeed, it can be said that the more something is small and seemingly insignificant in the eyes of the Judeo-Christian God, the more it seems to have value: "Whoever becomes humble like this child is the greatest in the kingdom of heaven" (Matthew 18:4). On this point, the great Judaic theologian, Abraham Heschel, is very emphatic:

> The Bible insists that God is concerned with everydayness, with the trivialities of life. The great challenge does not lie in organizing solemn demonstrations, but in how we manage the commonplace. The prominent feature of the biblical pattern of life is unassuming, unheroic, inconspicuous piety, the sanctification of trifles, attentiveness to details.[56]

Another thing we do well to keep in mind about polytheism is that it most often flourished not in primitive, nonliterate societies but in the "more advanced" literate cultures such as Greece, Rome, China, India and the ancient Near East (though there are some exceptions, such as in Mesoamerican and South American pre-Conquest religions, among the Yoruba people of West Africa and in Polynesia). The point is well made by Zwi Werblowsky, who sees a definite correlation between polytheism and those societies that have succeeded in distancing themselves from nature for their livelihood. He describes it thus:

The 'more advanced' cultures are those whose economy in some way provides sufficient surplus to create a certain distance between man and nature. Society no longer lives with its nose to the grindstone, so to speak. The result is increased division of labor (including bureaucracies and a priesthood), social stratification (including warrior castes, chieftains, royalty), and political structures (city, city-states, temple establishments, empires). Greek polytheism flourished in city-states; Mesopotamia (Sumer, Assyria, Babylonia) and Egypt were kingdoms and at times empires, and the same holds true of pre-Conquest Mesoamerica and Peru.[57]

Having made these preliminary observations about the polytheism of ancient history, we can now turn our attention to the present-day "return" of the gods and goddesses. At this point, the reader's first thought will perhaps turn to the contemporary idols we "revere/adore" today, especially in the world of sports, music or film, where the "Almighty Dollar" seems to take on all the attributes of a real, all-powerful God. Such an initial reaction would be understandable, given the huge sums of money we are prepared to pay our better athletes and celebrities today and the mass hero-worship that surrounds them. A case could easily be made that our exaggerated cult of sports heroes and film stars does indeed resemble the gods and goddesses of a Greek pantheon or shrine of old.

Hero-worship and personality cult are nothing new, of course, but they can have a dark and sinister side, where an individual is elevated to a pre-eminent status through a deliberate, well-planned propaganda campaign (Joseph Stalin in the 1930s and later Mao Tse-tung in China); through the movie industry's own "Best Picture of the Year" (the Oscars); through *Time* magazine's "Man of the Year"; and so on. A larger-than-life aura is then woven around such individuals, enticing adherents, inspiring followers and sometimes trapping ecstatic victims eager to emulate or give anything to their new heroes. We can get so wrapped up in our popular hero-worship that we want to know their opinion on just about everything, as though we expect an oracle from on high. It has been said that our heroes are the men and women who do things which we recognize with regret and sometimes with a secret shame that we ourselves cannot do.

At this point, I wish to dwell on a more subtle and less obvious form of contemporary polytheism than hero-worship. I will focus on the two principle areas where polytheistic thinking and imagining are emerging today – in the socio-cultural domain, on the one hand, and in the inner world of psychoanalysis, on the other. In both cases, it is important to remember that the present-day rebirth of the gods and goddesses is not to be taken literally. It is not a question of reviving dead gods, but rather a question of recognizing the polytheistic nature of the imagination and how the "gods" of old, though long dead, can still speak to us today in ways more subtle than we perhaps wish to acknowledge.

Polytheism: A Contemporary Root Metaphor

The fact cannot be ignored that in the last 20 years, polytheism has become a vibrant contemporary root metaphor. Not only has there been renewed interest in polytheism but serious attempts have been made to retrieve something of its lost wisdom in an effort to better understand our society and our times. I am thinking, for example, of the way feminist theologians are returning to the ancient goddess figures of mythology in an effort to liberate the Church from its sexist masculine bias. I am also thinking of recent studies such as those of historian David L. Miller in *The New Polytheism: Rebirth of the Gods and Goddesses,* of ethnologist Marc Augé's *Génie du paganisme,* of Edward Whitmont's *Return of the Goddess,* of Thomas Moore's popular *The Planets Within,* of David Fideler's studies on the polytheistic imagination and, of course, the revolutionary studies of psychologist James Hillman, to mention just a few.

In his study, David Miller argues that polytheism is alive and well in the contemporary world. Along with many others, he sees this as a good thing since it affords us "the opportunity of discovering new dimensions hidden in the depths of reality's history… a new freedom to acknowledge variousness and many-sidedness." For him, polytheism is a most appropriate metaphor for our contemporary society which is increasingly characterized by plurality – a plurality of values, of differing patterns of social organization, of principles by which we choose to govern our individual, social, political and religious life. He defines polytheism as "that reality

experienced by men and women when Truth cannot be articulated reflectively according to a single grammar, a single logic, or a
single symbol-system."[58] In contrast to monotheistic thinking,
polytheistic thinking has a feeling for the deep, pervasive and poten-
tially creative tensions that arise through our radical experience of
plurality in today's world.

The gods and goddesses of mythology, Miller contends, help
us in three ways. First, their arresting stories can open our eyes to
a new way of perceiving the multiple dimensions of everyday reality, whether it be the reality within us or that of the complex
world around us. Second, they can teach us greater tolerance in
accepting the ambiguity of our own diversity and that of others,
the ambiguity that increased plurality inevitably brings about. And
third, instead of viewing this plurality negatively – as fragmenta-
tion, chaos or potential anarchy – the polytheistic imagination gives
us a better sense of the richness and potency in the increasing
diversity and plurality that characterizes our society and our Church.
Seen in this perspective, then, the "return" of the gods constitutes
something of a subversion of the legacy of the Enlightenment in-
sofar as empiricism and scientific rationalism have belittled or neglected the legitimacy of imaginative thinking.

Mythologies have always been the result of creative imagination working on the experiences and facts of life. For us, in modern society, that means the experiences of several converging major trends: the growing autonomy of the individual as regards official institutions; the fact that people are increasingly assessing the
value of their beliefs in terms of their more immediate, everyday
needs; and the fact that the belief-systems of an increasing number
of people no longer refer to the kind of community in which
everyone thinks alike or is bound together as a result of sharing
the same interests, representations and practices. This is what Canadian sociologist Reginald Bibby, in his book *Fragmented Gods,*
has called "religion à la carte."[59] In a more recent work, *Unknown
Gods,* Bibby explores the possible reasons why there is an apparent
decline in religious participation in Canada and contends that one
of the major reasons is the slowness of the Churches to reflect the
social changes presently taking place in society. Because of this
"disconnectedness" from social evolution and change, a "spiritual

smorgasbord" ensues in which the God of the Bible takes its place and gets mixed up with the many other gods out there. Pollster Michael Adams, president of Environics Research Group and author of *Better Happy than Rich* and *Sex in the Snow*, has documented the profound social changes that have taken place in Canada in the past few decades. Among these changes is how the deference paid to patriarchal and institutional authority has plummeted; how Canadians desire greater autonomy and personal freedom; how money and material wealth matter less than personal worth; how Canadians are finding their own moral codes and reasoning out, for themselves, their own systems of ethics, as well as the right to live their lives in the ways they find most personally fulfilling. What this amounts to is the advent of a new pluralism, a new way of *being* Canadian, a new, more polytheistic way of thinking.

There was a time – before Vatican II – when monotheistic thinking prevailed in the Church's liturgy and theology. There was only *one* way to celebrate Mass, *one* unchanging language in which to rehearse it and *one* theology by which to interpret what was being celebrated, namely, scholastic theology. Today we are witnessing the birth of many "local" theologies – liberation theologies in Latin America, Asian theologies in the East, African theologies in Africa, etc. We are beginning to realize, as a bishop at the Second Vatican Council put it, that a Church with only one theology is a "dangerous Church."

Rehabilitating the Imagination

At the risk of oversimplification, it could be said that all this talk about the return of the gods and goddesses simply means that imagination and imaginative thinking are being reinstated in what has hitherto been an overly rationalistic way of thinking in the Western world. The real discovery today consists in seeing with new eyes, seeing imaginatively. The return of the gods and goddesses ushers in a new appreciation of imaginative thinking, which can be seen in such diverse fields as the philosophy of science, physics, sociology, anthropology and religious studies. If the twentieth century gave pride of place to rational thought, there is every reason to believe that the twenty-first century will be one of unprecedented imaginative thinking, with an ever-increasing number of new creative associations being made between what has hitherto been regarded as unrelated. No longer is imagination perceived as being opposed to perception and reason. Perception and reason are now understood as being continuously *informed* by the imagination. With the awareness that the imagination now performs a crucial mediating role in human experience, we have a better appreciation of the power and complexity of the unconscious and greater insight into the nature of archetypal pattern and meaning. The return of the gods and goddesses (like the resuscitation of our friend Lazarus) is challenging the fundamental assumptions underlying the paradigm of modernity.

By all accounts, we are experiencing a transition in history of epochal proportions, an "axial rupture" as some call it, namely, the radical breakdown of the modern paradigm. Like the foundations of a multi-storey edifice in the throes of collapse, all the basic assumptions of this paradigm are being called into question and no longer seem capable of seeing us safely through the new millennium. What are these assumptions that are eroding? As Charlene Spretnak and others have articulated them, they can be summarized as follows:

1. The belief in *unlimited progress.* Over and above everything else, progress must be pursued relentlessly in every sphere of life. If there is no sign of progress, then there is something definitely wrong which must be addressed and corrected.

2. The belief in the *exclusive supremacy of reason.* We must above all rely on objective rational thought. All other forms of "knowing" (e.g., intuition, affection, imagination, etc.) are suspect and must be treated as subjective and unreliable.

3. The belief in the *supreme autonomy of the individual.* The autonomous individual, relying on his or her inner resources and free will, is alone capable of self-development and self-fulfillment.

4. The belief in the ever-increasing *domination and control of nature.* Nature is perceived as completely subordinated to and under the complete control of human beings in the service of greater economic and industrial development.

5. The belief in *success and efficiency* as the true criteria for testing the real worth of any human endeavour, whether individual or

collective. Pragmatism, standardization and increased uniformity are seen as the most efficient way to insure happiness and economic development.

Every one of these major postulates of modernity is being seriously undermined today, and with their demise, the modern paradigm is imploding upon itself, like major construction that is being dynamited to make way for something new. Whenever a historical shift of this magnitude is experienced, the imagination comes prominently into the fray and seeks to envisage the construction of a new paradigm, a new heaven and a new earth. This is what we are witnessing today.

Our postmodern way of looking at reality is much more "inclined to be aesthetic rather than rational, more comfortable dealing with images than with ideas, inclined also to give direct subjective (even mystical) experience a validity that it seems to have lost some time ago."[60] This places all the various ways of knowing on a level playing field. With the new quantum physics, even the scientific community is beginning to recognize that "scientific progress" does not necessarily proceed in a rational manner, with a fixed inherent logic. In virtually every discipline, including theology and religious studies, it is recognized that the prodigious complexity and subtlety of reality far transcend the grasp of any one intellectual approach or particular "way" of knowing, and that only with a committed openness to the interplay of many perspectives can we meet the extraordinary challenges of our postmodern era. What is needed today is an approach that respects the multiplicity of *ways* of knowing "without recourse to a pre-established hierarchy of such mental acts."[61] What we need today, more than ever, is the ability to see and imagine a proliferation of unforeseeable possibilities.

The return of the gods and goddesses also means that in contrast to the scientist's quest for general laws defining a single objective reality, postmodern thinkers like James Hillman, Jean-François Lyotard and Scott Lash focus on the unbounded multiplicity of realities that continuously press in on our subjective awareness and on the complex uniqueness of each object, event and experience presented to us.

Hillman's Polytheistic Psychology

Let us now take a closer look at Hillman's "polytheistic psychology," which envisages the *inner sanctum* of our soul as the place where the gods are really said to dwell. Hillman's own approach to imagination has been informed by such thinkers as Edward Casey and Henri Corbin. From Casey, Hillman gains a phenomenology of the imagination, and from Corbin, Hillman adopts the notion of the *mundus imaginalis*, the imaginal world. For Hillman, the soul is, without doubt, the most crucial aspect of archetypal psychology. It is the mediating principle functioning between mind and body, subjective and objective, imaginal and rational, animate and inanimate. For Hillman, imagination is the primary activity of the soul, and he posits the soul, the seat of the imagination, as an intermediary between mind and body as well as between person and world. In this sense, the imaginal operates as a *tertium* between the personal unconscious and a person's consciousness; it also serves as a mediator between the personal and the impersonal, the individual and the world, the *anima mundi*. This places the soul, in the words of Thomas Moore, "midway between understanding and unconsciousness."[62] Thus conceived, the primary function of the soul is to connect the human with the non-human world, to integrate earth and sky, the gods and mortals.

In his seminal essay entitled "Psychology: Monotheistic or Polytheistic?" Hillman advocates a polytheistic paradigm in our psychological understanding of soul and introduces his basic contention with the following statement:

> By providing a divine background of personages and powers for each complex, it [a polytheistic psychology] would aim less at gathering them into a unity and more at integrating each fragment according to its own principle, giving each God its due over that proportion of consciousness, that symptom, complex, fantasy which calls for an archetypal background. It would accept the multiplicity of voices…without insisting upon unifying them into one figure, and accept too the dissociation process into diversity as equal in value to the coagulation process into unity. The pagan Gods and Goddesses would be restored to the psychological domain.[63]

Such a "re-visioning" of psychology has many implications. In what follows, I will not attempt to investigate or even distill the essence of Hillman's understanding of "polytheistic psychology." The reader can consult Hillman's many works on the subject, as well as those of his well-known soulmate, Thomas Moore. What I wish to do, instead, is simply highlight what I consider three of the more important benefits arising from this major paradigm shift in psychology. To do this, I will closely follow Hillman's own assessment.

(1) Reconnecting Psychology and Religion

The first thing that must be said about Hillman's polytheistic psychology is that, unlike traditional approaches, it explicitly reconnects the psyche with the sacred. By transposing, with the help of myths, what takes place in the human psyche into images of gods and goddesses, Hillman in fact resacralizes our traditional way of speaking about soul. He offers a sacred metaphoric backdrop against which we can begin to imagine the psyche in its multiplicity. In so doing, his polytheistic psychology offers a style of consciousness that disallows the strict separation of psychology and religion. He also repudiates all other dualistic separations, such as the mind from the body, rationalism from unconsciousness, self from other, gods from mortals, the animate from the inanimate. Hillman believes that the two, religion and psychology, are assumed by one another. As he puts it, "Psychology is always religious and theistic; theology, the study of the Gods, is always psychological." The difference between psychology and theology "lies not in our description of the Gods but in our actions regarding them."[64] In religion, he says, "Gods are *believed in*.... In archetypal psychology Gods are *imagined*.... They are formulated ambiguously, as metaphors for modes of experience and as numinous borderline persons."[65] By allowing the gods and goddesses to re-enter our soul-life where myths are forever being created, Hillman is thus able to sacralize what has hitherto been regarded as a purely secular domain in psychology and clinical therapy.

On this point, Hillman's thought is particularly important for the psychology of religion. In *The Myth of Analysis,* Hillman sees the Eros and Psyche myth as illuminating the process of psychological creativity. In particular, he sees Eros as the "missing link" to the realm of the gods and as the key which enables us to experience and participate in the imaginal world of the gods. The fact that Eros generally comes in the night is but another way of affirming the reality of contact with the divine, and Hillman considers this reality of divine contact as something that is experienced in the soul through the imagination.

(2) Accepting the Profound Divisions in the Soul

A second important aspect of polytheistic psychology is that it acknowledges and accepts as *normal* the essential and profound divisions in the soul – instead of viewing these divisions as some sort of psychotic dissociation in need of treatment and psychotherapy. Rather than making singleness of soul the norm, Hillman portrays the psyche as inherently multiple. "In Hillman's view," as Thomas Moore reads him, "we need a psychology that gives place to multiplicity, not demanding integration and other forms of unity, and at the same time offering a language adequate to the psyche that has many faces."[66] Indeed Hillman is critical of Carl Jung on this point and prefers a "polytheistic" psychology which recognizes that it is "the gods who clothe themselves in our complexes and speak through them."[67]

What Hillman is challenging here is the naive myth of normalcy. What is normal? And where do we get our criteria for judging what is normal? The normalcy fantasy, Hillman contends, becomes itself a distortion of the way things are. We all have complexes of one kind or other; we are all inherently "wounded" and vulnerable in our deep soul. And it is precisely this vulnerability, this deep "soul-wound," that Hillman posits as normal and generative of insight and a new way of seeing. From a Christian point of view, one is again reminded of St. Paul's confession: "I do not do the good I want, but the evil I do not want is what I do" (Romans 7:19). Hillman would see this as something normal rather than as a psychotic disorder. He would no doubt applaud St. Paul for recognizing and accepting his infirmities *(infirmitas)* as a profound and godly insight – a "blessing in disguise" – instead of repressing this infirmity or trying to escape or overcome it with conventional therapy. "Gladly will I glory in my infirmities," St. Paul says, "that the power of Christ may dwell in me" (2 Corinthians 12:9). This is why Hillman views pathology and insight as inextricably interwoven. "The wound and the eye are one and the same," he says. "Pathologizing is a way of seeing."[68] This also explains why the gods and goddesses of Greek mythology are so very important to us. For all their pathologies – their cheating, fighting, quarrelling, their sexual adventures and misadventures, their vulnerabilities, killings and tearing one another apart – the gods mirror our own human *infirmitas.* "Since the gods themselves show *infirmitas,* one path of the *imitatio dei* is through infirmity."[69] As a Christian, one cannot help but see here an echo of the Pauline notion of the Son of God's "self-emptying" (*kenosis*) and Jesus' own acceptance of being torn apart. One is also reminded of Henri Nouwen's insightful book entitled *The Wounded Healer.* That is precisely what the Greek gods and goddesses were, "wounded healers," and that is precisely what they invite us to become. My good friend and colleague Professor Ramon Martinez saw this clearly in his book *La Fragilité de Dieu,* as did William Placher in his work *Narratives of a Vulnerable God.* On this point, Hillman has every reason to remind us Christians of the following:

> If those concerned with the plight of religion would restore it to health and bring its God back to life, a first measure in this resuscitation would be to take back from the devil all the pathologies heaped on his head. If God has died, it was because of his own good health; he had lost touch with the intrinsic *infirmitas* of the archetype.[70]

(3) Celebrating Community with the World

A third and no less important contribution of polytheistic psychology is what the great Renaissance master of the inner life Marsilio Ficino called "the soul of the world," the *anima mundi.* By welcoming the Greek gods and goddesses into our soul, Hillman enlarges our hitherto restricted notion of soul. In traditional psychology and theology, we don't think of animals and plants as having souls, much less the cosmic world as a whole. Traditional psychology and its therapy have been almost exclusively centred on the personal development or growth of human individuals. Little or no consideration has been given to the subjectivity or soul of the world around us – that world in which we live and move and have our being, the world of things, plants and objects in which we are "embedded" and they in us.

For Hillman, not only plants and animals have soul, but soul is given to everything, even the "God-given things of nature and the man-made things of the street." Allow me to let Hillman speak for himself:

> The world comes with shapes, colours, atmospheres, textures – a display of self-presenting forms. All things show faces…. As expressive forms, things speak; they show the shape they are in. They announce themselves, bear witness to their presence:"Look, here we are." They regard us beyond how we may regard them, our perspectives, what we intend with them, and how we dispose of them. This imaginative claim on [our] attention bespeaks a world ensouled. More – our imaginative recognition, the childlike act of imagining the world, animates the world and returns it to soul.[71]

St. Francis of Assisi would surely have agreed wholeheartedly with Hillman on this score. He also viewed the world as "soul-filled," that is, possessing its own psychic depth and not just being a dumb collection of impersonal objects and "inanimate" matter. And if the world of things and the things of the world have subjectivity and soul, if every object bears witness to itself in the very image and face it presents to us, then it must follow – "as night the day" – that we also must entertain a most intimate, connatural and "soulful" relationship with them. Any therapy on our own soul, Hillman would argue, is ultimately ineffective without equal attention to the way the world bares its own soul to us. This *anima mundi,* or world soul, has its own areas of suffering, its own *infirmitas* that needs attention and caring: a severe "wound," we should hasten to add, that we humans have inflicted on Mother Nature. When we consider the enormous damage and pollution that we humans have inflicted on the planet's air, water and soil, and our exploitation of its natural life systems, we will need all the imagination and soul of the gods and goddesses to reverse this destructive trend. Only then may we begin to regain a deeper sense of intimacy with the living world around us, a world straining to be joined to us in a single community of existence.[72]

What is ultimately required, Hillman argues, is not a rational-istic response to this urgent challenge but an aesthetic one. Herein lies our capital sin, he would argue, namely, our lack of aesthetic response. To speak credibly today about either God or the soul, we must surely do so in terms of the beautiful. There is a deep and urgent longing in the human heart today for beauty, and this no doubt explains why the gods and goddesses are reappearing in our present day and age. In *The Thought of the Heart,* Hillman argues persuasively that it is necessary to reintroduce aesthetics to psy-chology: "We are led already to see that a full depth psychology expressing the nature of psyche must also be a depth aesthetics. Further, if we would recuperate the lost soul, which is after all the main aim of all depth psychology, we must recover our lost aes-thetic reactions, our sense of beauty."[73] As Hillman sees it, beauty is the supreme theophany, the divine revelation of the soul. Beauty is not simply a superficial attribute or quality of something; it is the manifestation of the soul itself and appears wherever soul appears. Beauty reflects the ways we are touched by the gods and god-desses, that is, by the heart. What is presented to our senses – the many faces of beauty and ugliness – entails spontaneous judgments made by the heart. Hillman argues that these aesthetic reactions, these spontaneous reactions of delight or disgust, should be seen as our primary initiation in moral responsibility. The question of ug-liness, therefore, like the question of evil we considered earlier, refers primarily to the anaesthetized heart. In either case, whether it is the face of beauty or the face of ugliness, the anaesthetized heart turns the living world into monotony, sameness and oneness. Hillman calls this the "desert of modernity," that place in our soul and in the soul of the world where we have effectively banished the presence of the gods and goddesses.

8

Imagination in Today's Spiritual Wilderness

He who does not seek God everywhere runs
the risk of not finding him anywhere.
—Vladimir Ghika

Ideas matter. One would only expect a professional theologian to say this, so let me hasten to add that ideas do not matter as much as the root images of reality which lie at the innermost core of our psyches and souls. A root image is our fundamental image of how reality is, our most basic "picture" of reality. It is an image with immense power since it not only provides a model of reality but also shapes our perception and our thinking. It has the singular function of serving as an imaginative inscape that affects all our seeing, thinking and acting. A root image or metaphor thus functions as both an image and a lens: it is a picture of reality which, in turn, becomes a lens through which we see and shape reality. This holds true for the way we "hold" and practise our faith in today's world, for the way we perceive Christian life and hence our personal commitment and involvement. Today, the root metaphor that best defines our situation as Catholic Christians in Canada and the United States is that of a *desert* or *wilderness*. In the concluding chapter of this study on the religious imagination, I wish to examine the vibrancy and dynamism of this biblical image, what this root metaphor means for us today, and how it can shape and creatively give rise to a new spirituality for our times.

Sojourn in the Wilderness

In the previous chapter, mention was made of the historical transition and radical change of paradigms we are presently experiencing. We indicated how the very assumptions and fundamental beliefs upon which the modern paradigm has been constructed are being seriously questioned and in many instances negated: the belief in *unlimited progress,* the unquestioning and quasi-exclusive *supremacy of reason,* the reckless *control and spoliation of nature,* the power of the *self-contained individual,* and the belief that *efficiency and success* are the measure of all things. Our quandary today is that we are in a "betwixt-and-between" situation, between a modern paradigm that is in decline and a new (postmodern?) one still in the making, a situation not altogether unlike what it must have been like during that transition period when the Middle Ages were in decline at the dawn of the Age of Enlightenment. On the one hand, the paradigm of modernity, which has served us well from the seventeenth century up until just a few short decades ago, shows every sign crumbling at its very foundations. We, the late moderns, can no longer trust what our ancestors held fast, especially the conviction that reason alone and increased knowledge can solve all of society's problems. On the other hand, it is still much too early to catch anything but a glimpse of what the so-called postmodern paradigm of the future will entail for all of us. It is inchoate and, therefore, still more of an expectation than a full-fledged historical reality.

It is my contention that our situation today is not unlike that of the Israelites after their liberation from Egypt and during their long sojourn in the wilderness. Egypt was "behind" them and the Promised Land was still a dream! Similarly, for all historical intents and purposes, the modern paradigm is "behind" us and as yet we can discern only dimly what the future may have in store for us. We are in a "betwixt-and-between" time, an historical wilderness, where nothing seems right or secure anymore: nothing seems to hold together as it once did. The most decisive feature of modernity in its declining stage, according to sociologist Anthony Giddens, is the growing uncertainty about its direction and its ability to get on the top of things and resolve some of the major social and economic problems it has created and left in its wake. In short, we can no longer subscribe to its basic assumptions. The radical nature of this historical shift in our time touches every aspect of our lives: the home, the family, the Church, the workplace, society, and all our institutions and cultural values. It is not an exaggeration to say that socially, culturally and religiously, we have entered a wilderness, and our desert experience, like that of the Israelites, will not be short-lived. Like it or not, we are here for the long-haul. In all likelihood, even our children and our children's children will only know and experience this unsettling, lengthy, transitional sojourn in the wilderness. Historical transitions between epochs, such as we are in, are never reckoned merely in years but in decades.

During such epochal transition periods, "axial ruptures" as Karl Rahner called them, there is always a lot of dislocation, rupture, discontinuity, protest and dissatisfaction. And with these dislocations, people tend to become polarized: some look upon the changing times as an opportunity, a blessing in disguise, a *kairos*; others see only gloom and doom, a lamentable time of crisis. This is to be expected. In our own day, there are those who want to return to the so-called "good old days," reminiscent of the discontented Israelites in the desert who longed to return to the "fleshpots" of Egypt. Already we can see that one of the characteristics of our time is the ascendancy of many conservative fundamentalist groups, both in religion and in society generally. Then there are those who reluctantly accept the inevitability of shifting times, but who "drop anchor," so to speak, who hunker down and seek security in what they consider *absolute* certitudes. They put their hope in the belief that the gale force winds of change will eventually pass and that things will in time get back to normal. Then there are those who refuse to cling to the past and who turn their sights steadfastly to the future; they are the restless ones, the young, especially, who are eager to push ahead and launch out into the deep. What we now see taking place is the baby boomers gradually being overtaken by Generation X and its successors, not unlike the scouts among the Israelites who went ahead of the people to explore unknown territory. And finally, there are those in the "silent majority" who don't quite know what to make of the present situation but who, nevertheless, strive to make the most of this new desert experience.

The symbolic imagery of the desert is itself a paradox and, as we have already noted, is also one of the most fertile "landscapes" in which our religious imagination can be set free and operate best. On the one hand, the desert conjures up a place of vulnerability, a place that is inhospitable, insufficient, desolate and barren, without much human appeal, a place, in fact, where we can easily get dehydrated, disoriented and lost. It is not a place for the faint-hearted but for those who like a challenge, who want to test their courage and endurance. On the other hand, with its vast horizons and wide expanses, the desert is a place of haunting wonder and awe, a place of extraordinary peace, tranquillity and beauty. It is a place where the brilliance of the sun plays its magic on the shimmering, whistling sands, where silence sings and where the sight of the moon and the stars, in the depth of their song, stirs wonder in the human soul. The desert is a place that invites contemplation and mystery, returns us to ourselves, and entices us to look *within* and to see *beyond* what meets the eye. In short, the desert becomes a "sacrament" in the powerful sense of this word, a physical landscape where the visible world reveals the proximity of an invisible world.

The desert or wilderness is also one of the most fertile images of Scripture. Here, too, we find the paradoxical "coincidence of opposites" between formidable hardship and amazing grace. The desert is territory that is frightening (Deuteronomy 1:19), desolate (Ezekiel 6:14) and murderous (Jeremiah 2:6). It is a place where faith is severely put to the test as nowhere else. It is in the desert where the people of God are summoned and must choose whether to put their trust in God or whether, grumbling and impatient, to return to Egypt. At the same time, it is also a place of purification, expectation and promise, a place where hope is born and set ablaze in the human soul. Throughout their 40 years in the desert, the Israelites were guided, protected and provided with food and drink by God – *one day at a time!* – thus creating sufficient space for hope to be born in the desert soul of Israel. The desert is not a place of refuge but a ritual passage, a threshold experience, a time in which we make God's promise our very own: to transform this desert into a garden, "He turns a desert into pools of water, a parched land into springs of water" (Psalm 107:35).[74]

If we accept the above analysis as a brief yet fair description of our changing times, and further, if we accept that this will be our "holding pattern" and *Zeitgeist* for some generations to come, then certain important consequences follow for the Church of the twenty-first century and the way we envisage our life of faith and spirituality. The remainder of this study will attempt to outline some of the salient features of what a spirituality for our present-day may look like. Using our God-given baptismal imagination, let us now try to envisage the major elements of a spirituality that is in keeping with the "signs of the time" and, therefore, one that is better suited for our sojourn in the wilderness.

(1) A Sense of Adventure

As narrated in the Bible, the first and most decisive feature of the desert experience is that it must be seen, read and re-enacted as an *adventure*. This was true of the Israelites' 40-year sojourn in the desert just as surely as it will characterize our own. Although the entire history of salvation can be read as a series of adventures with the God of Abraham, Isaac and Jacob and of Jesus Christ, there is a sense in which the desert experience, even in the life of Jesus, stands out as a unique and particularly harrowing adventure. It is one of the defining adventures between God and his people. It is an adventure in the most powerful sense of the word, and has all the necessary components to qualify it as such – so much so that this singular adventure in the desert has become the privileged metaphor for all subsequent "close encounters" with God.

What is an adventure? What is it about an adventure that makes it different from other human undertakings? And what might change if our life of faith were seen more as an *adventure* with the living Spirit of God than a faith to "cling" to and to merely "pass" on to the next generation, like a baton in a relay race? Christopher Kiesling sums up well what a real adventure is all about:

> The word adventure connotes a positive undertaking, like discovering the source of the Nile or scaling Mount Everest. It involves struggling to meet challenges: limited human resources, diseases, difficult or dangerous terrain, extremes of heat and cold. In meeting challenges there are advances and reverses, successes and failures. Adventure entails planning ingeniously, mustering courage, attempting, falling, revising strategy, renewing courage, trying again, and persevering...until the goal is reached. The outcome of the adventure is uncertain, the final attempt at the goal may fail. Adventure means taking risks and requires daring, courage, patience and perseverance....Adventure is stimulating and exciting; it gives zest to life and a feeling of satisfaction.[75]

This is a pretty fair description of the inner dispositions that a new spirituality would have us embrace in our present-day wilderness: a lively sense of adventure. The 40-year sojourn of the Israelites in the desert was undoubtedly an adventure, one that will forever stand out as "unforgettable" in the Judeo-Christian tradition and liturgy. Clearly, an adventure such as this is fraught with many dangers and uncertainties. It is a time when one needs a lot of perseverance and trust in the Lord of history; it is a time of temptation and a time of purification, a time for soul-searching and a time for bonding, for forging community. Since both life and faith are a never-ending vocation and our stance before God is always an ongoing process, the crucial thing is not so much whether we succeed or not, but whether we live the venture as though our destiny depended on it, with as much flexibility and fortitude as possible. Nothing can be taken for granted in an adventure. "Success" and "efficiency," we said, were the hallmarks of the modern paradigm, as well as a former spirituality. Today, we experience our faith odyssey much more in terms of an "arduous venture," not unlike the declaration of the great twelfth-century mystic Richard of St. Victor: "What if I do not reach the goal I strive for? What if I falter in running the course? Well, I will nevertheless have had the joy of having run, labored and sweated as much as I could in search for the face of my Lord."[76]

The spirituality of our parents and grandparents will not suffice to see us through our present-day wilderness. A new spirituality is needed. In this new spirituality, I am suggesting, the life of faith will not be construed primarily as a fixed, unchanging "deposit" of doctrine but more as an adventure with God's unpredictable way of loving us in today's world. It will be a spirituality that does not emphasize obedience at the cost of creativity, or unquestioning loyalty to tradition that risks missing the Lord who is just now coming to meet us in today's world. Our challenge is to envisage our faith more as an *odyssey*, a genuine adventure, where the stakes are high and the outcome is never a foregone conclusion. It will be a spirituality that is ever mindful of the risk that St. Paul spoke of, namely, a keen awareness that if Christ is not risen, then even our best efforts will have been in vain (1 Corinthians 15:17). It will be a spirituality, in short, that recognizes the inherent gamble in every act of faith, and hence will urge and prompt us to resolutely go out on the proverbial "limb" because that is where the fruit grows. To use Bonhoeffer's apt expression, it will be a "costly grace" because it entails putting ourselves "on the line" for others; it entails a venture that involves more personal risk than security, more ambiguity than clarity, more contingency than order, more questions and doubts than ready-made answers. It should be noted, too, that none of these are necessarily a sign of a weak or diminished faith; much less are they contrary to genuine faith. The only sign of being of "little faith" is fear itself, as Jesus frequently reminded his close circle of friends and disciples. It will be the very same faith that marked those who went before us, but it will be experienced quite differently. Our desert spirituality will prepare us to accept the irruption of something new, something unforeseeable and unpredictable in the world we live in, especially the inscrutable ways God makes his presence, absence and love known to us in the present-day "axial rupture" of our times. We will perhaps even learn to "sing a *new* song to the Lord," a song that will be much more "in tune" with our times and therefore unlike any other raised up to God. In the final analysis, what really counts in an adventure with God, especially in the desert wilderness, is to continue to believe in the Risen Lord who provides enough reason to hope – but in fact *only* for hope.

If all of this sounds too abstract and theoretical, let us consult the laity and ask them to describe, in their own words, how they would describe their faith experience in today's world. With few exceptions, they invariably describe it in terms of a difficult and challenging experience, with many of the connotations and elements we normally associate with a genuine adventure. Here are just a few typical responses gleaned from recent conversations I have had with some of my immediate acquaintances:

- "You wouldn't believe what I've been through! If it wasn't for my faith in God, I wouldn't have made it this far."
- "Keeping the faith is no problem; living it in today's world is the real challenge."
- "I've come to realize that my faith is not a security blanket. It doesn't make life easier, just more demanding."
- "You ask about my life of faith? I see it as a continuous struggle, especially with my conscience."
- "I try to say my prayers every day, but I wish God would speak to me more often and not be so silent."
- "My personal life of faith? It's like taking two steps forward and one step back."
- "Things get very confusing at times, but I just try to follow my conscience and hope for the best."
- "'Man proposes and God disposes' – isn't that what they say? When it's all over, maybe I'll be able to look back and say: 'I can see more clearly now!'"

Such utterances could well have fallen from the lips of most Israelites during their sojourn in the desert. In fact, many believers today increasingly find themselves on a similar wilderness venture. What many believers are beginning to realize is that the traditional image our parents and grandparents had of God no longer corresponds to their efforts of trying "to seek his face" in today's world. The real question, therefore, is not so much whether people are losing their faith but whether or not the Church today is capable, like a New Moses, of entering *with its people* into this wilderness. Is the Church capable of projecting, in its preaching, proclamation and media exposure, an image of God that corresponds to the laity's actual experience of God in today's world? Is the Church capable of *interpreting* Scripture in such a way that she, too, can *imagine* the God of biblical revelation as forever young instead of old, forever adventurous instead of staid, forever challenging instead of repetitious? In short, can the Church imagine and proclaim a God who is forever eager to strike out on yet another new venture with his people? Is it conceivable that a *new* venture with God is in the offing and that what we need to re-imagine, instead of the staid God of classical theism, is the God of Abraham, Isaac and Jacob, the God of Jesus Christ, as One who is still vigorous, full of life and is ever ready to change his mind and embark on some new adventure with those he loves? Are we dealing with a God who can change his mind or "relent" – as Scripture has it – and who never forsakes his people when they need him most? Is this an adventurous God who is always the *first* to put his prevenient love "on the line" and in so doing, derives enormous delight in taking yet another divine risk on our behalf? In short, is it too much to image that God is eager to begin writing another new chapter in the story of his abounding love for his people and this world?

(2) **Learning to Appropriate Our Fragility**

Another feature of our desert experience is that it gives us an increased sense of vulnerability. Everything changes in the wilderness, including the way we perceive our world, ourselves, our faith and God. We begin to see things through the lens of fragility rather than of power, vulnerability rather than of self-reliance and ambiguity rather than of certitude. Even our notion of what is sacred changes in the wilderness. Under the secular paradigm of modernity, the Church has had to settle for a diminished role and place in the public arena, and religion has become increasingly privatized. As a result, most of us have grown up with what I call an overly "solid" and restricted sense of what is sacred: we have come to equate "sacredness" with worship and anything that has to do with the Church, ritual performance or God. Sacredness came to be defined almost exclusively in the restricted ritual sense we spoke of earlier in Chapter 4, that is, as something "set apart" from the profane and specifically dedicated to the service of the Church and divine worship. In this sense, paradoxically, the sacred became more visibly *distinct* in our secular society: The church was regarded as a sacred building; its sanctuary as a most sacred area; its priests as sacred ministers; and the icons, statues, vestments and vessels used in the celebration of the Mass were also considered sacred. Sunday, of course, was the sacred day of the week par excellence, as were the major seasons and feasts of the Church's calendar. Thus the sacred "stood out" in marked contrast to the secular and was visibly distinguished from the profane. Indeed, it was a "sacredness" of only *certain* places, things and people.

In the desert, this historic "betwixt-and-between" era in which we now find ourselves, we see and define the sacred differently. A spirituality that sustains and nourishes us during our desert odyssey will be one that allows us to search for and find God in places, times and situations other than the sanctuary of the Church and its sacred rites. Vladimir Ghika, whose quote opened this chapter, was a Romanian prince who became a Catholic priest and died a martyr in a Communist concentration camp in 1954. His words are particularly apt for us today as we begin our own odyssey in a new wilderness: "He who does not seek God everywhere runs the risk of not finding him anywhere." The good news in this advice, as St. Bernard and other great mystics remind us, is that "No one can seek you, O Lord, who has not already found you." Or as St. Gregory of Nyssa put it: "To find God means to search for him without end."

Not only will we come to experience the truth of that timely paradox in the years to come but we will discover that God does indeed let himself be sought *and* found in every new historical era, even (perhaps especially!) in those great axial ruptures in history such as ours. Our new spirituality will remind and reassure us that God is still Emmanuel, that is, still very much "with us" in the wilderness, and that he is not any farther removed from us today than he was when we were totally ensconced in the paradigm of modernity some 50 years ago. Using our creative religious imagination, our new spirituality will re-interpret for us, albeit from a different perspective and in a different cultural context, what our Christian forebears used to call "Divine Providence." We will come to know that the kingdom of God is still very much "at hand," even in our changing world.

Today and increasingly in the years to come – with an ever-keener sense of our individual and collective vulnerability, contingency, poverty and fragility – our "solid" definitions and fully reliable categories of the past will give way to another, more inculturated spirituality. Fragility, not strength, now becomes the lens through which we view reality, including the way we perceive and name what is sacred in our new surroundings. With the loss of much of what we hitherto have considered "solid" ground, the desert expands our vision, our urgent longings and our "classical" definitions. In the desert, where the religious imagination is once again resuscitated and set free – like Lazarus of old – our sense of the sacred takes on an altogether new dimension beyond its former restricted meaning: sacredness now becomes "everydayness." *Every* day becomes sacred; *every* creature, great and small, becomes sacred; *every* hour, place and person takes on a sacred aura and hence the potential for a "close encounter" with God. In the desert, the distinction between the sacred and the profane disappears, and sacredness is seen as an inherent quality of everything that is. As we learn to appropriate our vulnerability, fragility and dependency, everything suddenly takes on a sacred quality, whether the smallest drop of water or the most insignificant of God's creatures. We begin to view everything we come across as a *companion* desert-dweller. We experience what Victor Turner calls *communitas*, that is, a new and unprecedented way of relating to one another as equals, as fellow-travellers who are in the process of assuming our common status and poverty. And with this new sensibility there emerges a new way of searching for and relating to God.

In the previous chapter, we saw that a God of infinite love is not so much an almighty, all-powerful God as a vulnerable God, and that love by its very nature makes one vulnerable – indeed the more loving, the more vulnerable! Today we can relate to this much more readily than in the past. Fragility and vulnerability now become our privileged way of envisaging reality, the lens through which we understand ourselves, our world, our Church and our God. Perhaps the best indication of this perspective is the new collective awareness regarding the rights and dignity of the child, that most telling symbol of vulnerability and gift – vulnerable because a child is fragile and can so easily be hurt or injured, and gift because we see the promise of our own future in the face of every child. No wonder then that at this critical turning point in our history, our collective imagination would have us embrace the innocent Child who will save us all.

Pablo Picasso once remarked that "it takes a long time to become young." And Jesus said that "whoever does not receive the kingdom of God as a little child will never enter it" (Mark 10:15). In either case, a lot of imagination is required to capture something of the eternal childlikeness of God. God's eternal Word is given to us as a child and this Child-Word, vulnerable and deprived of power like every child, can only be captured by a youthful soul. It is quite possible to be a little old man or woman at the age of 21, just as it is possible to retain a youthful heart forever. What ultimately defines youth or old age is the age of one's soul – not the body – and the years of a soul are invariably measured by what/whom it loves. Hence the sound advice of St. Augustine: "O you that are young, if you would remain young, seek Christ."[77] In our longing for a lost innocence or childhood, our religious imagination is our great baptismal gift that forever entices us to be abundantly alive to God's promises and tense with expectation. What ultimately makes a youthful soul is its capacity to hope and to love everything.

To believe in the God of the gospel, the God of Jesus, is to believe in the possibility of something new. A God who discreetly "sings in the night" more readily than in the broad daylight of empirical evidence, a God who does not always wish to be encountered in exactly the same place or the same time, will invariably make his presence known at the most inappropriate times and in the most unforeseeable circumstances. He will make unheard-of demands, and will inspire us to new forms of adoration and as-yet-untried ways of approaching him. Is this not what the psalmist had in mind when he urged us to "sing a new song to the Lord!"? While the "new" does have the uncanny ability to initially trouble and disconcert us, it should not unduly disturb those who have faith. It will only trouble those of "little faith," those whom, like the disciples, Jesus rebuked during the storm at sea: "Why are you afraid, you of little faith?" (Matthew 8:26). Christian faith is not incompatible with human worries and anxieties, only with fear. The reluctance to face the "new" out of fear is contrary to Christian faith because the God of biblical revelation is forever creating something new: "See, I am making all things new" (Revelation 21:5). This means that while we are in the wilderness, our prayer to the Holy Spirit should correspond to a readiness to accept the unpredictable, the surprising, the new. The Holy Spirit does not provide prescriptions we merely need to fill. To invoke the Holy Spirit requires boldness, risk-taking, the courage to live with paradox and to venture forth in confidence, without having all the answers. The desert is the birthplace of hope precisely because there are no clearly indicated paths or road signs. As the great Spanish poet Antonio Machado put it, a road is nothing more than the footsteps we leave behind us:

> Traveller, there is no road,
> Walking is what makes the road.
> And when we look behind us
> We can then see the path
> We'll never have to walk in again.[78]

The imagination is always invigorated and captivated by new ideas that call into question the limitations and confining boundaries within which we have comfortably become ensconced, if not imprisoned. If the imagination has a vocation, in connivance with the mission of the Holy Spirit, it is surely to liberate us today, as in every age, from those mental and structural boundaries that so often make us resort to repression and injustice in order to justify our entrenched mindsets. In reality, this only serves to reinforce as sacrosanct those social, political and religious boundaries we set up. This even holds true for the Church as an ecclesiastical institution, as Leonardo Boff quite rightly states:

> *The Spirit is the divine imagination.* It will not be hemmed in. It is the mobility of the church, its ongoing disinstallation, its dissatisfaction with itself, stimulating it to ever new efforts along the pathways of all people.[79]

When we hear a word of hope, we hear it first and foremost at the level of the imagination. Jesus' proclamation of the kingdom of God in our day and age is no exception. It presents real possibilities that we could never entertain were it not for the Holy Spirit, that is, God's own divine imagination and the imaginative dimension of faith itself. Why is this? Because what is at stake here is a kingdom or reign in which the last somehow become the first, the poor are somehow recognized and heralded as the "blessed" ones of God, the despised and oppressed are the real prophets and "good Samaritans" of our day, and the improbable prospect that even the "prodigals" in our world today will be reinstated and lavishly celebrated in this kingdom. Is it possible to imagine a peaceable kingdom right here in our cities, towns and neighbourhoods, where a lion and a lamb can live together side-by-side – and do so, moreover, without the lion losing anything of its beautiful wild nature or the lamb, anything of its meekness? What cannot possibly happen does indeed happen in God's kingdom! When depicting this kingdom with his own parabolic imagination, Jesus challenges us "to say what cannot be said, to applaud what should not be applauded, [and] to recognize in the reversal of human judgements and human situations the signs of the breaking in of God's Kingdom."[80]

As a power and posture of the soul, imagination is all-inclusive and leaves nothing "untouched." It can embrace and be in communion with anything under and beyond the sun. Nothing – absolutely nothing! – is beyond its reach, familiarity or communion. It can take unto itself anything that is known or unknown, insignificant or important, present or absent, material or spiritual, mundane or godly, on earth or in heaven. The reason for this extraordinary power of intimacy, this power "to love everything," lies in the fact that the imagination dwells in the landscape of the soul where borders are fluid and permeable, not divisive and obtrusive, where life emerges nowhere as fully and deeply as when borders and frontiers are crossed. Like our friend Lazarus, imagination stands at a point of intersection between this world and the next, between time and eternity, light and dark, life and death, anticipation and fulfillment. With this threshold advantage, our religious imagination accompanies us at every step and turn of our faith odyssey in the wilderness.

(3) New Interconnections

Another important feature of our emerging spirituality in the desert resides in our enhanced perception of the "bigger picture" and the possibility, therefore, of discovering the relationships and interconnections between things that have thus far escaped us. In the modern paradigm, the tendency was to "fragment" the various spheres of life and reality into clearly separate domains. The basic metaphor through which we perceived reality was that of the "machine": on the other hand, we thought of everything as somehow made up of autonomous, independent parts, and we became quite skilled in naming and differentiating these many parts. Today, on the other hand, we are much more aware that interrelatedness is basic to the universe. Our older certitudes about time, space and matter have changed. Physicists now tell us that the ultimate particle of matter might not be a solid but a wave of energy, with the result that the language of natural laws is giving way to talk about sets of relationships. The new emerging metaphor today is one of wholeness and interconnectedness wherein everything hangs together – for better *and* for worse – as in a huge, intricate "spider's web." Our vision is expanded in the desert and we naturally begin to take notice of the whole, which is always greater than the sum of the parts. Paradoxically, since the whole is contained in each part and since no whole is ever complete in itself, the inherent connections between things now become for us even more important than the individual parts considered in and of themselves alone. We could call this the "betweenness" of things, that is, the view that everything is related to everything else. This new way of "seeing" reality in its interconnections is precisely what the imagination does best, as we saw earlier in Chapter 4. It is also conditioned and enhanced by the very fact that we ourselves now live in this "betwixt-and-between" transitional period in history. Thus it comes as no surprise that the focus of so much attention and study today centres precisely on the inherent connections between science and religion, body and soul, objectivity and subjectivity, *eros* and *agape*, terrestrial and celestial, human and divine, sacred and profane.

We do not have to look very far for signs of this profound shift in our thinking about the reality of the world, the self and the nature of divine reality. It is corroborated by the systems theories in modern science and the quantum theory in physics. These new theories are pushing both the scientific imagination and the religious imagination to new frontiers. Tony Kelly, in his important work *An Expanding Theology: Faith in a World of Connections*, has attempted to draw out some of the profound implications of this for theology today, as has Linda Olds in her book *Metaphors of Interconnectedness*. Worthy of mention here are the many scholarly studies undertaken by David Ray Griffin, founder of the Center for a Postmodern World, and the series of works published by the State University of New York on constructive postmodern thought such as *Sacred Interconnections: Postmodern Spirituality, Political Economy, and Art*. There can be little doubt that a growing number of Christians in North America today join in this new spiritual outlook. It may not always be at a reflective, conscious level, but it is certainly experienced at the level of "affective intentionality" (Tallon), that is, the affective consciousness of feelings and moods deep within the soul: hence the present-day fascination with Eastern mysticism and new paths of spirituality, with the gods and goddesses of old, with angels; the deep affinity between the feminist movement and the ecological movement ("Eco-feminism"); the renewed interest in "alternative" medicine; and the proliferation of religious publications dealing with various aspects of the "betweenness" of things. Without any promotional effort on the part of the Church, the great mystics of our own Christian tradition are being rediscovered and their writings republished and read. The twelfth-century German mystic Hildegard of Bingen is a case in point. Like many others, her remarkable sensitivity enabled her to gain deep insight into the forces and energies in nature, their co-penetration and interdependence in the universe. "Everything that is in the heavens, on the earth, and under the earth," she wrote, "is penetrated with connectedness, penetrated with relatedness."[81]

The religious imagination is very much "at home" in such a web-making spirituality. The current re-emergence and presence of angels in our imaginations, thoughts and bookstores is an indication of this. Why angels? Because angels enable us to express certain phenomena we would otherwise be quite unable to utter except in symbolic form. They are a fluid and subtle symbol of God's own gracious presence to his people, the appearance and likeness of his radiant glory. The idea of angels also represents the psychic forces within the human spirit itself and, in another sense, those forces that impinge upon the human spirit from without. Furthermore, they are what we could call "go-between" or "connective" beings; they serve to join things visible and invisible, material and spiritual, the human and the divine. The mission of these "extra-terrestrial" visitors is precisely to enable us to see reality in its connectedness rather than in fragments. We gave the Devil his due in Chapter 6; so here would be the obvious place to trace the iconography of angels.

As with demons, angels have also been variously depicted in different centuries, at times undergoing significant representational changes. Their reappearance today, along with the resuscitation of our friend Lazarus, is an indication that a new spirituality is in the making. Nor is there any indication that people are in a hurry to clip the wings of these celestial messengers. Recognizing our vulnerability in the desert wilderness, we begin to speak differently, listen differently and behave differently. We also willingly take all the help and assistance we can get.

Our ideas about God are always culturally conditioned, as Vatican II made plain, and when we viewed the world as a "machine," we imaged God from within that perspective. Now our plight in the desert wilderness impinges upon our religious imagination and affords us a new understanding of God. Now we realize that God's plan for our universe and for our Church is much more complex than we used to think. We need a spirituality today that takes into account this complexity and our precariousness in the wilderness. For on this journey, we will need to make generous allowance for the virtue of flexibility, that nimbleness of spirit which alone prevents us from getting disheartened by the surprises that a venturing God may have in store for us in the wilderness. Even the aging Cardinal Ratzinger, head of the Sacred Congregation for the Doctrine of the Faith and one of the more unbending figures at the Vatican, recently urged Catholics to be flexible. He reminded us that Jesus and his disciples had shown flexibility in their actions and teachings at the dawn of Christianity. What is needed in any desert experience is flexibility, or what the French call *le dynamique du provisoire,* the ability to seize the moment and make the most of every passing opportunity. Like the Israelites of old, we will learn to live our hope-filled faith *one day at a time* – as though it were our *first* and *only* day with the Lord of the Wilderness.

Epilogue:
Dare We Imagine?

Is it too much to imagine, as Pope John Paul II suggested, that we might think of God as having a "feminine side" and hence as being our Mother? "The hands of God hold us up," he said, "they hold us tight, they give us strength. But at the same time they give us comfort, they console and caress us. They are the hands of a father and a mother at the same time."[82]

Is it too difficult to imagine that when Christ redeemed our world through his incarnation, passion, death and resurrection, he not only saved us human beings but also every living and non-living creature on Earth? Must we continue to think of the Incarnation as having taken place solely for our *human* benefit and species, or can we imagine that the Son of God has effectively united himself in some fashion with all created reality?

Dare we imagine that even our favourite animals, both wild and domestic, will somehow join us in the hereafter? And that since every dandelion, blade of grass, insect and bird is endowed with soul, ought they not also to return to their Creator to sing his eternal praise and glory?

Are we wrong to think that even some of our best theologians have been far too parsimonious and restrictive in the way they have made us look upon Christ's saving and redemptive grace? If God were seen to be too generous, too lavish or too wildly extravagant in bestowing his "amazing grace" on all creatures great and small, far beyond the visible boundaries of the Church, would it somehow cheapen divine grace, make it less "sacred" and, therefore, less precious and appreciated?

Is it too much to imagine, furthermore, that God may well have peopled the stars and outer planets with soul and intelligent life? That we humans may not be the sole heirs of his divine revelation, providence and bountiful love? Or that God's idea of an ongoing creation and an expanding universe might far exceed even our most reliable scientific observations?

When we think of the Holy Spirit, that divine helper sent down upon the earth and Church after the resurrection of Our Lord, dare we imagine that this is in fact God's very own divine imagination, still groaning in the soul of the world to bring about a new heaven and a new earth? That his divine imagination and our own religious imagination do indeed have an uncommon, providential affinity? Dare we give ourselves permission to imagine that even organized religion, as we know it, has yet to discover the true face and heart of God? Has yet to envisage less timidly and celebrate more vibrantly "the breadth and length and height and depth" of Christ's love, and experience this love which surpasses all knowledge? (Ephesians 3:18-19)

And finally – or is this, also, not something too good to be true? – dare we imagine that Our Lord was not exaggerating when he said, "Truly, I tell you, as often as you did it to the least of my brethren, you did it to me"? Or that the "sacrament" of the neighbour is just as *real* a sacrament, just as efficacious, as the Eucharist, and one that places the kingdom of God, like the Eucharist, quite literally in our midst – indeed, at our very fingertips?

A paradox is defined as a seemingly absurd or self-contradictory statement, although one that may harbour a profound truth. As French theologian Henri de Lubac reminds us:

> Paradoxes are paradoxical: they make sport of the usual and reasonable rule of not being allowed to be *against* as well as *for* [something]. Yet, unlike dialectics, they do not involve the clever turning of *for* into *against*. Neither are they only a conditioning of the one by the other. They are the simultaneity of the one and the other. They are even something more – lacking which, moreover, they would only be vulgar contradictions. They do not sin against logic, whose laws remain inviolable: but they escape its domain.[83]

Kierkegaard believed that "one should not think slightingly of the paradoxical; for the paradox is *the source of the thinker's passion, and the thinker without a paradox is like a lover without feeling: a paltry mediocrity.*"[84] Some of our greatest spiritual writers and mystics, those passionate men and women in our Christian tradition who ardently strove to experience God "up close and personal," have all resorted to the use of paradox to describe what these encounters were like. The veracity of their testimony is rarely in doubt since it is supported by the acknowledged holiness of their lives. Yet it requires considerable religious imagination on our part to appropriate their mystical utterances and begin to appreciate for ourselves the deep wisdom contained in their paradoxical statements about God. I close this study with several such paradoxical statements and invite the reader to stretch his or her faithful imagination to see to what extent the following paradoxes resonate within you.

I put these paradoxes to the reader in the form of a question – "Do you believe...?" – as a final summation of the importance of the religious imagination in our desert spirituality:

Do you believe, with Pierre de Berulle, that God "is infinitely present and infinitely distant, infinitely elevated and infinitely close to us, infinitely desirable and infinitely insupportable"?

Do you believe theologians who reassure us that we can know God and those, like St. Augustine, who tell us that if we think we know God, it is not him?

Do you believe the biblical book of Exodus when it affirms that no one can see God and live?

Do you believe that St. Leo the Great was not altogether wrong when he says that the person who presumes to have found what he/she has been looking for has not found it, but has failed in their search?

Do you believe the great mystic St. Bernard when he says, "No one can seek you, O Lord, who has not already found you"?

Do you believe William of St. Thierry, who echoes St. Bernard when he says, "No one truly seeks you [God] without finding you because the very truth that you are being sought contains in itself the unexpected answer of a truth that has been discovered already"?

Do you believe the great German spiritual master Meister Eckhart when he says, "Not to be able to reach God is our discovery; the failure itself is our success"?

Do you believe St. Catherine of Genoa when she tells us that the souls in purgatory endure their sufferings so willingly that "the excess of their joy does not remove the smallest part of their suffering, nor the excess of their suffering the smallest part of their joy"?

Do you believe that St. Augustine got it right when he affirms quite categorically that "Every creature is an image of the Creator, although nothing resembles God"?

Do you believe the English mystic Julian of Norwich when she says that "Our Saviour is our true Mother"?

Do you believe that the monk Thomas Merton may have seen something we miss when he states, "The more perfect faith is, the darker it becomes"?

Do you believe Léon Bloy, the French "Pilgrim of the Absolute," when he warns us: "If a person gives a poor man a penny grudgingly, that penny pierces the poor man's hand, falls, pierces the earth, bores holes in suns, crosses the firmament and jeopardizes the entire universe"?

Do you believe that Mechtild of Magdeburg, considered the greatest German female mystic of the Middle Ages, tells us something important when she declares that "the soul is just as safe in the body as in the kingdom of Heaven"?

Do you believe this other holy woman, Margaret Porete, who declares that "the soul does not get drunk on what it imbibes, but gets drunk and very intoxicated on precisely what it has not drunk and will never drink"?

Do you believe there might be a grain of truth in the words of Blessed Angela of Foligno when she says, "In our eyes there are many who appear to be condemned unto hell, but who are saved in the eyes of God, and many in our judgment who appear to be saved yet who are reprobate in the sight of God and condemned unto hell"?

Do you believe Jesus when he tells the crowd on the mountainside, "Blessed are you who are poor, for yours is the kingdom of God"? (Luke 6:20)

If some of these mystical utterances resonate within you, dear reader, you are in good company indeed. And what is more, you will have just exercised your religious imagination and baptismal right. Don't stop now! Our sojourn in the wilderness has just begun.

Notes

[1] Blaise Pascal, *Pensées,* trans. H.F. Stewart (London, 1950), 39.

[2] Jacques Le Goff, *The Medieval Imagination,* trans. Arthur Goldhammer (Chicago: The University of Chicago Press, 1988), 5, 6.

[3] Sharon Parks, *The Critical Years: Young Adults and the Search for Meaning, Faith, and Commitment* (San Francisco: Harper, 1991), 117.

[4] James E. Loder, *The Transforming Moment: Understanding Convictional Experiences* (San Francisco: Harper & Row, 1981), 32.

[5] Marcus J. Borg, *The God We Never Knew: Beyond Dogmatic Religion to a More Authentic Contemporary Faith* (San Francisco: Harper, 1997).

[6] Andrew M. Greeley, "Good liturgy is little more than a good weave" in *National Catholic Reporter,* March 16, 1990, 12.

[7] Roger Haight, *Dynamics of Theology* (New York: Paulist Press, 1990), 154.

[8] Quoted in Keith F. Pecklers, *The Unread Vision: The Liturgical Movement in the United States of America: 1926–1955* (Collegeville: The Liturgical Press, 1998), 217.

[9] The tally breaks down as follows: 14 on the Way of the Cross, 1 above the sanctuary, 4 on the presider's alb, 1 on the processional cross, 4 on the altar palladium, 23 in the stained glass windows, 1 on the ambo, 1 on the paschal candle, 1 on the tabernacle door, and 46 on the side of each church pew.

[10] Thomas Merton, *Disputed Questions* (New York: Farrar, Straus and Cudahy, 1960), 155, in his chapter "Sacred Art and the Spiritual Life."

[11] Pope John Paul II, "Letter to Artists," in *L'Osservatore Romano,* 28 April 1999 [special insert], p. II, no. 10.

[12] Pope Paul VI, "L'Église et l'art," in *La Documentation catholique, 61* (1964), 686-687. [author's translation]

[13] Hans Urs von Balthasar, *The Glory of the Lord,* Vol. 1 (San Francisco: Ignatius Press, 1982), 18-19. [Italics added.]

[14] St. Thomas Aquinas, *In I Sent. Prol.,* q. I, a.v.

[15] Bernard of Clairvaux, *On the Song of Songs* (Kalamazoo, MI: Cistercian Publications, 1980), trans. Irene Edmonds, Sermon 74, 89-91.

[16] See Karl Rahner, *The Practice of Faith: A Handbook of Contemporary Spirituality* (New York: Crossroad, 1986), eds. Karl Lehmann and Albert Raffelt, 77-84.

[17] Quoted in Olivier Clement, *The Roots of Christian Mysticism* (London: New City, 1993), 246.

[18] Leon Bloy, *Pilgrim of the Absolute,* ed. Raissa Maritain (New York: Pantheon Books, 1947), 83.

[19] Teresa of Avila, "The Interior Castle," Chap. 1:i, in *The Collected Works of St. Teresa of Avila,* Vol. 2, trans. Kieran Kavanaugh and Otilio Rodriguez (Washington, DC: ICS Publications, 1980), 283.

[20] For an in-depth study of this controversy, see "Images & Contemplation," in *Dictionnaire de Spiritualité*, tome VII, 2 (Paris: Beauchesne, 1971), especially col. 1490–1503.

[21] Thomas Merton, *New Seeds of Contemplation* (New York: New Direction Books, 1961), 134.

[22] Eulallo R. Baltazar, *The Dark Center: A Process Theology of Blackness* (New York: Paulist Press, 1973), whose insights I am deeply appreciative of in what follows.

[23] John O'Donohue, *Anam Cara: A Book of Celtic Wisdom* (New York: Cliff Street Books, 1997), 145.

[24] Robert L. Cohn, *The Shape of Sacred Space: Four Biblical Studies* (Chico, CA: Scholars Press, 1981).

[25] Beldon C. Lane, *Landscapes of the Sacred: Geography and Narrative in American Spirituality* (New York: Paulist Press, 1988).

[26] *Sacred Places and Profane Spaces: Essays in the Geographics of Judaism, Christianaity, and Islam,* eds. Jamie Scott & Paul Simpson-Housley (New York: Greenwood Press, 1991).

[27] Ronald Bordessa, "The Iconic Self: Luther, Culture, and Landscape in Finland," in *Sacred Places and Profane Spaces,* eds. Jamie Scott & Paul Simpson-Housley, (New York: Greenwood Press, 1991), 90.

[28] For the most compelling studies in this field, see Wyman H. Herendeen, *From Landscape to Literature: The River and Myth of Geography* (Pittsburgh: Duquesne University Press, 1986); Simon Schama, *Landscape and Memory* (New York: Alfred A. Knopf, 1995).

[29] *Sacred Places and Profane Spaces,* xiv. For an excellent study of visionary imagination in the Middle Ages, see Aaron Gurevich, *Historical Anthropology of the Middle Ages* (Chicago: University of Chicago Press, 1992), 65-89.

[30] Philip Porter and Fred Lukermann, "The Geography of Utopia," in *Geographics of the Mind* (New York: Oxford University Press, 1976), 199.

[31] Quoted by Yi-Fu Tuan, "Geopiety: A Theme in Man's Attachment to Nature and to Place," in *Geographies of the Mind,* ed. David Lowenthal (New York: Oxford University Press, 1976), 33.

[32] Pierre Berton, *The National Dream and The Last Spike* (Toronto: McClelland & Stewart, 1974), 22.

[33] Edmond Barbotin, *The Humanity of Man* (Maryknoll, NY: Orbis Books, 1975), 43. I have substituted the word "road" for his original "route."

[34] Acts 9:2; 18:25f; 19:9; 22:4; 24:14.

[35] Gaston Bachelard, *Water and Dreams: An Essay on the Imagination of Matter* (Dallas: The Pegasus Foundation, 1942), 16.

[36] Paul Valéry, *The Collected Works of Paul Valery,* ed. Jackson Mathews, Vol. 7, tr. Denise Folliot (New York: Pantheon Books, 1958), 80.

[37] Quoted by his sister in the introduction of his *Thus Spake Zarathustra,* in *The Philosophy of Nietzsche* (New York: Modern Library, 1954), xix-xxxiii.

[38] Yehudi Menuhin, *Theme and Variations* (New York: Stein and Day, 1972), 9.

[39] *Summa Theologica,* q.60, a.3c.

[40] Eugene O'Neill, *Nine Plays* (New York: Garden City Publishing, 1940), 418.

[41] For a most accessible account of the mystery plays and how they were staged, see Alice K. Turner, *The History of Hell* (New York: Harcourt Brace & Company, 1993), 114-125.

[42] Aron Gurevich, *Medieval Popular Culture: Problems of Belief and Perception* (Cambridge: Cambridge University Press, 1990), 180.

[43] Ibid, 10.

[44] St. Robert Bellarmine, *Hell and Its Torments* (Rockford, IL: Tan Books & Publishers, 1990), 42.

[45] Richard Younge, *A Serious and Pathetic Description of Heaven and Hell, According to the Pencil of the Holy Ghost* (London, 1672), 4-5.

[46] Henceforth the word "devil" will appear in lower case to signal a change in the devil's stature in our modern technological society.

[47] Eric Voegelin, "Immortality: Experience and Symbol," in *Harvard Theological Review,* LX (1967), 237.

[48] Mary Douglas, "The devil vanishes," in *The Tablet* (28 April 1990), 513.

[49] Karl Rahner, "The Devil," in *Sacramentum Mundi,* Vol. 2 (London: Burns & Oates, 1968), 74.

[50] Roger Haight, *Dynamics of Theology* (New York: Paulist Press, 1990), 154.

[51] John Macquarrie, *Principles of Christian Theology* (New York: Charles Scribner's Sons, 1977), 238.

[52] *Concilium,* Vol. 1, 1998.

[53] Kenneth L. Woodward, *Making Saints: How the Catholic Church Determines Who Becomes a Saint, Who Doesn't, and Why* (Simon & Schuster, 1990), 93-94.

[54] Joseph Campbell, *Myths to Live By* (New York: Viking Press, 1972), 214-215.

[55] Pierre Teilhard de Chardin, *The Phenomenon of Man* (London: Collins, 1959), 257.

[56] Abraham Heschel, *The Insecurity of Freedom* (New York: Schocken Books, 1972), 102-103.

[57] R. J. Zwi Werblowsky, "Polytheism," in *The Encyclopedia of Religion,* ed. Mircea Eliade (New York: Macmillan, 1998), Vol. 11, 438.

[58] David L. Miller, *The New Polytheism: Rebirth of the Gods and Goddesses* (New York: Harper and Row, 1974), 4.

[59] Reginald Bibby, *Fragmented Gods: The Poverty and Potential of Religion in Canada* (Toronto: Irwin Publishing, 1987), 62.

[60] Bernie Neville, "The Charms of Hermes: Hillman, Lyotard, and the Postmodern Condition" in *Journal of Analytical Psychology* 37 (2), 39.

[61] Edward Casey, *Imagining: A Phenomonological Study* (Bloomington, IN: Indiana University Press, 2002).

[62] Thomas Moore, *Care of the Soul: A Guide for Cultivating Depth and Sacredness in Everyday Life* (San Francisco: HarperPerennial, 1992), xiii.

[63] James Hillman, "Psychology: Monotheistic or Polytheistic?" in *Spring* (1991), 193-208, 230-232.

[64] James Hillman, *Re-Visioning Psychology* (New York: HarperPerennial, 1975), 169.

[65] Ibid. [Italics added.]

[66] James Hillman, *A Blue Fire,* ed. Thomas Moore, (New York: Harper & Row, 1989), 37.

[67] James Hillman, *The Dream and the Underworld* (New York: Harper, 1979), 129.

[68] Ibid., 149.

[69] Ibid., 151.

[70] Ibid.

[71] James Hillman, *The Thought of the Heart and the Soul of the World* (Woodstock, Connecticut: Spring Publications, 1992), 101-102.

[72] For an insightful and visionary study of this issue, see Thomas Berry, *The Great Work: Our Way into the Future* (New York: Bell Tower, 1999).

[73] James Hillman, *The Thoughts of the Heart,* Eranos Lecture Series 2 (Dallas: Spring Publications, 1981), 26.

[74] See also Isaiah 32:15; 35:1-7; 41:18; 51:3.

[75] Christopher Kiesling, *Celibacy, Prayer and Friendship* (New York: Alba House, 1978), 65.

[76] Richard of St. Victor, *De Trinitate,* 1.iii.

[77] St. Augustine, *Ad fratres in eremo,* Sermon 44. [*Quaerite, O juvenes, Christum, ut juvens maneatis.*]

[78] *"Caminante, no hay camino,/Al andar se hace camino/Y al volver la vista atras/ Se ve la senda que nunca/ se ha de volver a pisar."* – Antonio Machado. [my translation]

[79] Leonardo Boff, *New Evangelization: Good News to the Poor* (Maryknoll, NY: Orbis Books, 1991), 86. [Italics added.]

[80] Norman Perrin, *The New Testament: An Introduction* (New York: Harcourt Brace Jovanovich, 1974), 295.

[81] Quoted in Diarmuid O'Murchu, *Reclaiming Spirituality: A New Spiritual Framework for Today's World* (New York: Crossroad, 1998), 84.

[82] Pope John Paul II, General Audience, 8 September 1999.

[83] Henri de Lubac, *Further Paradoxes,* trans. Ernest Beaumont (Westminster, MD: The Newman Press, 1958), 76.

[84] Soren Kierkegaard, *Philosophical Fragments,* trans. Howard V. Hong (Princeton, NJ: Princeton University Press, 1962), 46. [Italics added.]

A Short Bibliography

Alison, James. *Raising Abel: The Recovery of the Eschatologial Imagination*. New York: Crossroad Publishing Company, 1996.

Avens, Roberts. *Imagination: A Way Toward Western Nirvana*. Washington, DC: University Press of America, 1979.

Brann, E.T.H. *The World of the Imagination: Sum and Substance*. Savage, MD: Rowan & Littlefield, 1991.

Boff, Leonardo. *New Evangelization: Good News to the Poor*. New York: Orbis Books, 1991.

Bohm, David. *On Creativity,* ed. Lee Nichol. New York: Routledge, 1989.

Bryant, David J. *Faith and the Play of Imagination: On the Role of Imagination in Religion*. Macon, GA: Mercer University Press, 1989.

Calasso, Roberto. *Literature and the Gods*. New York: Alfred A. Knopf, 2001.

Cocking, J.M. *Imagination: A Study in the History of Ideas*. London: Routledge, 1991.

Egan, K. & D. Nadaner, eds. *Imagination and Education*. Milton Keynes, UK: Open University Press, 1998.

Engell, James. *The Creative Imagination: Enlightenment to Romanticism*. Cambridge: Harvard University Press, 1981.

Erickson, Carolly. *The Medieval Vision: Essays in History and Perception.* New York: Oxford University Press, 1976.

Fingesten, Peter. *The Eclipse of Symbolism.* Columbia, SC: University of South Carolina Press, 1970.

Fisher, Kathleen R. *The Inner Rainbow: The Imagination in Christian Life.* New York: Paulist Press, 1983.

Freedberg, David. *The Power of Images: Studies in the History and Theory of Response.* Chicago: The University of Chicago Press, 1989.

Greeley, Andrew. *The Catholic Imagination.* Los Angeles: University of California Press, 2000.

Green, Garrett. *Imagining God: Theology and Religious Imagination.* San Francisco: Harper & Row, 1989.

Gregory, Derek. *Geographical Imaginations.* Cambridge, MA: Blackwell, 1994.

Herendeen, Wyman H. *From Landscape to Literature: The River and the Myth of Geography.* Pittsburgh: Duquesne University Press, 1986.

Hillman, James. *The Myth of Analysis: Three Essays in Archetypal Psychology.* New York: HarperCollins Publishers, 1972.

Hillman, James. *The Force of Character and the Lasting Life.* New York: Random House, 1999.

Kaufman, Gordon Dester. *The Theological Imagination: Constructing the Concept of God.* Philadelphia: Westminster Press, 1981.

Kearney, R. *The Wake of Imagination: Ideas of Creativity in Western Culture.* London: Hutchinson, 1988.

Ladd, George W. *Imagination in Research: An Economist View.* Ames, IA: Iowa State University Press, 1987.

Lane, Beldon C. *Landscapes of the Sacred: Geography and Narrative in American Spirituality.* New York: Paulist Press, 1988.

Le Goff, Jacques. *The Medieval Imagination,* ed. Arthur Goldhammer. Chicago: The University of Chicago Press, 1988.

Mackey, James, ed. *Religious Imagination.* Edinburgh: Edinburgh University Press, 1986.

McIntyre, John. *Faith, Theology and Imagination.* Edinburgh: Handsel Press, 1987.

O'Donohue, John. *Anam Cara: A Book of Celtic Wisdom.* New York: Cliff Street Books, 1997.

Ricoeur, Paul. *Rule of Metaphor: Multidisciplinary Studies of the Creation of Meaning in Language,* trans. Robert Czerny et al. Toronto: University of Toronto Press, 1981.

Robinson, Edward. *The Language of Mystery.* London: SCM Press, 1987.

Schama, Simon. *Landscape and Memory.* New York: Alfred A. Knopf, 1995.

Thiemann, Ronald F. "Revelation and Imaginative Construction," *Journal of Religion,* #61 (1981): 242-243.

Tierney, Nathan. *Imagination and Ethical Ideals.* Albany: State University of New York Press, 1994.

Tracy, David. *The Analogical Imagination: Christian Theology and the Culture of Pluralism.* New York: Crossroad, 1981.

Warnock, Mary. *Imagination.* Berkeley and Los Angeles: University of California Press, 1976.

Webb, Stephen H. *Blessed Excess: Religion and the Hyperbolic Imagination.* Albany: State University of New York Press, 1993.

Ulanov, Ann and Barry. *The Healing Imagination: The Meeting of Psyche and Soul.* New York: Paulist Press, 1991.

White, A.R. *The Language of Imagination.* Oxford: Blackwell, 1990.

AGMV Marquis

MEMBRE DE SCABRINI MEDIA

Québec, Canada
2003